AF572022

LIVE, BELOVED, LIVE

Wellness Begins Inside

DR. ROBBIN ALSTON

Archway Publishing books may be ordered through booksellers or by contacting:

Archway Publishing
1663 Liberty Drive
Bloomington, IN 47403
www.archwaypublishing.com
844-669-3957

Interior Graphics/Art Credit: Malcolm Alston

ISBN: 978-1-6657-3594-0 (sc)
ISBN: 978-1-6657-3595-7 (hc)
ISBN: 978-1-6657-3593-3 (e)

Library of Congress Control Number: 2022923934

Print information available on the last page.

Archway Publishing rev. date: 5/5/2023

Dedication

To my Ancestors of antiquity for making,
it possible for me to be.
To my mother, Dorothea Barnes, despite her struggles,
and premature death, who choose me to be.
To the following bloodline who left this world much too
early. It's because of you, I write *Wellness Begins Inside*.
I promise, as a descendant and benefactor of your life
to be responsible and continue on the path of purpose
and build upon the foundation you have laid before me.
I am inspired. May your light guide me. Àse.
To all the spirits of our individual families, known and
unknown, and whom we silently remember in our heart.
We praise and honor you. Àse,

Edward Alston-Barnes
Thomas Barnes
Franchot Barnes
Joshua Barnes
Alvin Barnes
Kate Barnes
Mark Barnes
Regina Kirby-Barnes
Rita Barnes
James Barnes

ACKNOWLEDGMENT

Food is crucial to whatever we want to do in life. So, what we choose to eat is no small matter. Unfortunately, we only change our eating habits when we get sick, a diagnosis, or someone we know is ill. In my life, it was both. As a food-deprived child and later cancer survivor, I realized that something had to change for me to live. That change came out of awareness that food is not merely what we eat but life itself. And so, strengthened with awareness, I decided to go on a healing journey. When I did, I met some fantastic individuals who brought out of me this uncompromising urge to care about what went inside my body and to see food as a first responder to healing. These people profoundly impacted my quest for wellness through food and cooking. I have drawn much inspiration and knowledge from these exceptional individuals, who have molded me into a mindful cook and transformed my life. Through the many books I've read and under the teachings of others, I became inspired to pursue the healing process to reverse diseases and halt genetic ailments. It is a spiritual process for which I am eternally grateful to others.

I wish to thank Dr. Muata Ashby, Dr. Llaila Afrika, Dr. Earl Mindell, Dr. Edward Bach, Kenneth S. Cohen, Dr. Andrew Weil, Edgar Cayce, Jonell Nash, Harish Johari, Amadea Morningstar, Urmila Desai, and Ptahhotep. I wish to thank

Sister Gail Stevens for her expertise and patience and for gifting me with my first cookbook. I want to express special thanks to Sister Gloria for allowing me to sit in her kitchen and watch her bake bread. I no longer call her delicious, whole-wheat golden-brown rolls-biscuits. And I still cherish the vintage glass candy cooking thermometer she handed down to me for baking bread. I wish to acknowledge Atiya Ola for her wise words and humility regarding food. And I thank all the fantastic chefs, gardeners, and vegetables and fruit merchants that have crossed my path, either in the street, grocery stores, kitchens, or restaurants in the United States and abroad. To the Village Produce Merchants, thank you for making available the best-seeded watermelons. To all the health warriors whose wisdom I carry within me, I am grateful.

No book is written without the unwavering support, perseveration, and encouragement of others. And so, due to the energy and inspiration of a few amazing people in my life, *Wellness Begins Inside* is born. I wish to thank Malcolm Alston, my son, who is a constant flow of inspiration and motivation. He never fails to challenge me to go further, to Rita Hart, whose words of encouragement and her continuous appreciation for my creative dishes always energize me. A special thank you to Hunter Landon for the many hours spent reading and rereading, analyzing the numbers, and enjoying the many dishes cooked, but above all, for his faith in *Wellness Begins Inside.*

As I grow and evolve, I am eternally grateful to God and my ancestors. With every breath I take, may I use them wisely.

DISCLAIMER

This book provides general information and discussions about health and food related subjects. The information and other content provided in this book, or in any linked materials, are not intended and should not be construed as medical advice, nor is the information a substitute for professional medical expertise or treatment and is not meant to give specific recommendation of advice for treatment of particular illnesses.

If you or any other person has a medical concern, you should consult with your health care provider or seek other professional medical treatment. Never disregard professional medical advice or delay in seeking it because of something that you have read on this book. If you think you may have a medical emergency, call your doctor or emergency services immediately.

The opinions and views expressed on this book have no relation to those of any academic, hospital, health practice or other institution.

Your food is supposed to be your medicine, and your medicine is supposed to be your food. —African Proverb

CONTENTS

PREFACE

Born into poverty in the streets of Washington, D.C., I claim no grand lineage or privileged entry into this world. I am merely the lone descendant of deceased parents and over ten siblings. Nonetheless, I bring to you plenty of experience in sickness, illnesses, and death, but also inspiration in changing our eating habits, lifestyle, environments and unblocking our energy. The way we choose to live is not done in a vacuum. Everything we do, such as what we eat and how we eat, comes from somewhere. Our childhood conditioning lays the groundwork for our later choices in life. If unhealthy choices surround us, we will choose unhealthy choices as adults. Like all children, I merely ate what I was given at the time, mostly corn starch. I carry no shame in admitting that corn starch kept me alive temporarily.

For some of us, these were devastating times. Eighty-nine years after the end of slavery, which was the time, I came into this world as an destitute child in the late '50s- corn starch quieted my belly. Life circumstances exposed me to three life-threatening diseases: polio, smallpox, tuberculosis, and another less-talked-about disease that stalked me: malnutrition. Like children you see on those hunger relief commercials, I was one of the million underweight colored children suffering from food intake and nutrient deficiencies right here in the United States. Malnutrition is cruel; it left a calling card, inflicting me with nutritional-deficiency anemia and arthritis in my early life. I shout with gratitude to all four corners of the earth; I am alive despite the unchanging impoverishment and diseases, standing guard at any moment to shorten my life only because of what I have learned.

I lived my first three years of life off and on in the streets deprived of food with the exception of cornstarch Eventually, taken off the streets, I was placed in an institutional setting and later in housing with certain foods that were difficult to digest, such as meat and oatmeal. While no longer being starch-fed, now I was forced to eat all my food, even if it was undigestible, in an emotionally charged environment. Food, in many ways, became a frenemy, a friend, and a foe. Since some foods didn't agree with me, I hid it, preferring to not eat. Along with my complicated tryst with food, emotions were forming, leading me down an unhealthy path.

Nothing altered my unhealthy lifestyle for years. That is until I was diagnosed with breast cancer. Cancer compelled me to think about life. Four-millimeter cancer cells roaming within my body took me on an inward journey. Suddenly, I found myself struggling not only to live but also to fulfill my dream of completing my doctoral studies in psychology. But now, right, midway through my studies, I bump into cancer. All of a sudden, nothing else mattered but life. As a child, I'd lost my mother and didn't want my son to lose me. Admittedly, I was terrified. Often, we talk about spirituality, but when we're faced with death and doctors have reached their limit, spirituality becomes our only recourse in fighting to live.

Even though I was suffering mentally, seeking mental health wasn't the answer. I shied away from western psychology labeling machinery. Nor did I believe the paradigm of the West could understand this fear mixed with disappointment and anger that resided within me. Besides, I didn't want a diagnosis but healing. So, I began to dig deeper into my life and connected with my spirit, which led me to my unconscious way of living. With consciousness, I learned that my diseases grew not just from the foods I ate but from my attitude, thoughts, and misunderstandings blocking my energy or life force. Cancer in me was not this conglomeration of large, dark cells but a mental and spiritual force.

Interestingly, we don't think about life until it is threatened. In an article, I wrote for Essence magazine, "I am a Breast Cancer Survivor" I made this point by saying,

"I no longer take life for granted after that diagnosis. It is indeed a gift and not a guarantee. My healing has begun now, and I have taken up life's challenges to live truly." This fight knocked me on the rope in the ring of life by taking me back to my childhood, where I realized that my earlier fainting and, later, regurgitating were food-mind-spirit disorders from unresolved emotions in my life. Cancer forced me to dig deep and start healing.

When I did, I started arming myself by changing my food choices and adopting spiritual practices, including meditation, yoga, breathing exercises, qigong, self-study, cooking, and gardening. In doing so, slowly, I began releasing a lot of emotional clutter in the form of misunderstanding.

Second, I realize I am alive with over sixty years of experience because I chose understanding over a misunderstanding, self-care over carelessness, and gratitude over shame. That's right; I used to feel shame about the conditions I was born into until I understood them. *Wellness Begins Inside* enables us to transform ourselves with the power of understanding. Often, what we don't understand, we ignore or neglect. Understanding, however, facilitates mindfulness, healing, and even transformation. Essentially, this book reminds us to heed the messages from our experiences to understand why we eat the way we do, live the way we do, and sometimes act contrary to life.

Wellness Begins Inside starts with a personal food story because everyone has one. Rather than judge our food choices, we reveal our stories. What are our earliest food memories? How were we introduced to food? Was there a feeling of scarcity or denial? Of unpleasant emotions and worry? Is it one of joy and abundance? Our past experiences surrounding food tell a story. We might find that we eat the way we feel about ourselves. These feelings, which are negatively charged, often result in many of us succumbing to diseases and premature death—not so much because of genetics but lifestyle and misunderstanding. However, this changes when we look at our food story and understand it.

Today, there is an abundance of books, lectures, and even documentaries on food and nutrition at our disposal. Earlier in my life, this knowledge wasn't readily available to me. Yet, in the face of looming death, my healing journey connected me with a plethora of knowledge and extraordinary cooks, healers, and the healed. As a psychologist, educator, cook, and yogini, I've learned that becoming healthy includes what we eat but also a spiritual and mental way of life. While current medical messaging puts a great deal of emphasis on nourishing the body and dieting. We're much more. Health is the science of right living, the nature of food, but also understanding ourselves. Food, as well as thoughts, spiritual practice and rituals, reenergizes the body, mind, and spirit. Ultimately, being healthy is an energy practice intricately linked to our purpose in life.

What is your purpose? As a breast cancer survivor and the only remaining member of my immediate family, my purpose, in part, is to share my transformation, insights, and wisdom in this book. It hasn't been easy but necessary. Along the way, some doctors have frustrated me with *their* tendency to pre-diagnose me with my family diseases. I often left their offices with traces of hopelessness. My fate was sealed after they heard about the deaths of my family members without considering that my lifestyle differed. One of my brothers suggested that I stop giving the doctor background information instead of making them work for it by getting to know me. I understood the reasoning behind their pre-diagnosis, but I also knew my family's lifestyles.

Many doctors did not consider that I was a vegan and lived differently than the gene pool I was born into. All I wanted the doctors to do was consider my lifestyle and refrain from cursing me with an unmanifested disease by pre-pilling me. One doctor flippantly said, "You're African-American, so that you will have high blood pressure; I am white and will probably get osteoporosis. I didn't return.

Of course, I've also met some excellent doctors who communicated with me and supported my healing journey. I could relate the sketchy information about my family history without the usual reaction—still, these interactions emphasized the importance of self-care and working collaboratively with your doctor. Besides, the science of epigenetics informs us that our behavior and environment impact our health as well-it's just not our genes. If so, opening the Àse Yoga Studio & Tea Room, cooking all of my meals using fresh organic fruits and vegetables, practicing yoga and qi gong, gardening, and meditating should impact my health favorably.

We don't have a say over the gene pool we come through, but neither do we have to sustain that genetic lifestyle. *Wellness Begins Inside* came from my realization that I am not my family's disease. Also, from my struggles and witnessing too many unnecessary or preventable diseases and deaths. If only we paid more attention to what's happening inside us, I wondered. If only we connect to our internal organs as much as we do to the external world, perhaps we could reduce some of the chronic diseases brought on by our lifestyle. Clearly, our way of living is powerful. But I've learned so are we. This book speaks to reclaiming our power from food but also unhealthy experiences. It's not enough to share our experiences; we must realize the potency lies in understanding them.

I invite you on this life-affirming journey with the hope that you realize that our health depends on the choices we make. When our consciousness is awakened, we change our choices and engage in actions that transform our lives. Awaken your consciousness-make health and healing a priority. Let's live life to the fullest, where diseases no longer dominate or occupy our lives. Let's live to heal.

May you *Wellness Begins Inside*
Dr. Alston

INTRODUCTION

Her name is Health; she is the daughter of Exercise,
who begot her of Temperance. The rose blusheth
on her cheeks, the sweetness of the morning
breatheth from her lips; joy, tempered with innocence
and modesty, sparkleth in her eyes and from the
cheerfulness of her heart she singeth as she walketh"
- Ancient Egyptian proverb

These pragmatic verses offer insight into Ancient Egypt's understanding that exercise and temperance serve as conduits to Health. We find ample evidence from the extensive writings of Dr. Muata Ashby that from the pre-historic period, around 25,000 to 35,000 B.C.E., our ancestors realized the nature of Health. They had uncovered elements which include exercise and moderation as ways toward health. However, things changed, it seems that starting around the 20th-century, with the inventions of the radio, electric, refrigeration, the radio, and television; overeating became a primary cause of weight gain and unhealthiness. And so, Ill-temperance, not temperance, became our way.

Just think with all the information on health, and weight loss plans, thousands of years ago, our ancestors discovered the way. Ignoring what was already known, as the years have passed, we've engaged in the antithesis of health by practicing sedentarism and ill-temperance. Meanwhile, nothing dominates our conversations more than ill-health or our ailments—except pictureperhaps money. And despite what we know about health, we mindlessly practice ill-health to the detriment of life. I was one of those people who mindlessly ate and lived unaware until I experienced an awakening through cancer.

That awakening is open to all of us. To facilitate it, *Wellness Begins Inside* starts us off on a journey into the story of our personal food: experience; the foundation of our food choices. Then it calls our attention to the *why*, *what*, *when*, *where,* and the way of food. Why do we eat? No doubt our typical response to this question would be "To live" or "Because we're hungry." It might surprise you to know we eat for other reasons. Sometimes, we're not biologically hungry, yet we eat. In those instances, we may be living to eat and not eating to live. We're feeding our emotions at the expense of our health. *In Wellness Begins Inside*, we uncover the actual reasons we eat.

Are you eating real food? There's no "why" without a "what." Rather than calling it "junk" or "fake" food, we should call it what it is: poison. Poison is any substance capable of causing illness or death when introduced to or absorbed by a living organism. Indeed, none of us would knowingly poison ourselves. However, with our consumption of the six FDA-approved dyes, 2,500 fine chemicals, genetically engineered food, salt, and added sugar, we may be doing just that. Are we knowingly poisoning ourselves with the over 8,948 to almost 47,000 food choices at our disposal? Of course not, but it's happening.

Where does this poisoning take place? Is it in our cars, offices, beds, or homes? Do we eat at our desks or outside our homes? Do we eat at a table? What about intermittently looking at our cell phones while eating in front of our televisions? Does it even matter where we eat? Research suggests that it matters because where we eat impacts our digestive system, cholesterol levels, cardiovascular health, and overall health.

The next question is: When does this damage happen? Is it during breakfast, lunch, or dinner? While a few of us still subscribe to the seventeenth-century European settlers' traditional model of having breakfast, lunch, and dinner at specific times, others enjoy brunch—a combination of late-morning breakfast and lunch. Are you one of those people that skip breakfast, lunch, or dinner and eat randomly? Does it even matter, when we eat? Are we designed to eat on a twenty-four-hour cycle? Does it matter if we eat late at night because we work late? The answers may be a cause for you to pause.

The way we eat is different from the way we used to eat. Indeed, technology, modernism, and cultural shifting have changed how we eat, from shoving food into our mouths without chewing to eating while walking outside. Distracted eating due to our cell phones, blue screens, or televisions is typical. Some of us even use our bellies as a table by setting our plates on our bellies to eat. Do we eat with our hands? Do we bypass saying a prayer of gratitude before eating? Do we eat as a family, with friends, strangers, or solo? Over the years, our ways of eating have changed from family style to fast style.

Wellness Begins Inside, ask these questions and respond to them to empower and encourage us on our health journey. Covering areas creating the most harm, we put the four silent health defendants on trial: salt, sugar, saturated fat, and stress. No longer can we ignore them since they are the leading offenders in our ill health. The good news is that we can now read how much of these offenders are in our food.

Nutritional labels flank the items we buy, giving us informed consent when purchasing food? Do you read the nutritional labels? How do you decide whether or not to buy the product? Solely by taste or nutritional content?

Food is in varying quantity and quality around us. Of course, some people have limited access to affordable and nutritious food, which is called a food desert. In contrast, others have higher access to better supermarkets or fresh vegetable shops known as food oasis. Of course, there is no denying that food deserts are a significant problem. But even people that have access are choosing heavily, nutritionally insufficient, or empty foods. So, both inaccessibility and poor choices affect the quality of our lives. As someone who ate corn starch to survive and was born before even the food stamp programs, I know the feeling of the desert. I also know what it feels like to have a choice but choose unwisely. We can only minimize, and even reverse food-choice illnesses derived from our lifestyle by making wise choices.

By now, you know that regardless of our economic status, degrees, and positions we hold, none of us are immune to being sick or in ill health. If the recent pandemic taught us anything, it is that our other conditions—such as cancer; chronic kidney, liver, and lung disease; neurological conditions; and diabetes (type 1 or type 2)—heightens the harm., If we're suffering from heart conditions, a weakened immune system, obesity, or physical inactivity, the only way to reduce further complications and possibly save our lives is to become healthy. As we do, we experience health as the "sparkleth in her eyes and from the cheerfulness of her heart she singeth as she walketh."

Unlike most books on health, this book reflects my *lived but also learned experience*s. It's not about eating this, not eating that, or even dieting. Instead, it is about healing. To do that,

Wellness Begins Inside does something unique it appeals to us to examine our own lives, to awaken our consciousness so that we live before we die. In this book, we do that by being aware of self-care and adopting the C.U.P mindset. All that we learn become Reflections, which turn into Revelations that emphasize the importance of going beyond the surface, the body, to understand and transform our actions. A section on tea is included because it's restorative and encourages us to slow down. Make sickness history and wellness your present. Go from dis-ease to ease, from illness to wellness, from overweight to a healthy weight, and from fast food to healthy food. Health is attainable when we practice self-love by taking care of ourselves with exercise, moderation, understanding, and knowledge. I am alive to share *Wellness Begins Inside* because of all of this and more. Be well.

FOOD STORY

Each moment I am alive becomes a realization
that every discomfort, disease, and disappointment
I experienced was an opportunity for me to
understand myself and heal." -Dr. Robbin Alston

Within any book, a story exists. *Wellness Begins Inside* is no different, except this is a food story. Food stories bring to light the reasoning behind our food choices and eating habits. The purpose of *Wellness Begins Inside* is to challenge us to reflect on our stories, understand them, and transform our lifestyles into ones that exude healthiness and healing. We do that by uncovering deeply buried wounds and misunderstandings, sustaining our unhealthiness. We use the term unhealthy to mean a state of imbalance, dis-ease, or illness. Health and healing go together. An African proverb says it best "We have to heal the wound before it ignores the medicine."

Let's heal our wounds by understanding our experiences. I won't inundate you with ancient secrets, an overabundance of research, or even tribal wisdom. Instead, I'll tell you a story because stories are indispensable to our healing. Stories serve as reservoirs for our feelings and conditionings that govern how we live. When we understand our stories, we change our experiences and transform our lives. I'll go first with bringing my food story to you. Here is my food story:

Once upon a time, a little colored girl was born into starvation, which triggered several illnesses. That girl was me. Street life had taken its toll on my frail body. I was the host for malnourishment and dis-eases like smallpox, anemia, influenza, arthritis, and tuberculosis, putting me in imminent danger.

Early on, I'm told, my food consisted of only breast milk. Then, the breast milk dried up as I grew and gave way to corn starch, a white, hard, crunchy substance. This starch is used as a food thickening thickener and in adhesives in paper products, anti-sticking agents, and textile manufacturing. As a result, I suffered from anemia and iron deficiency and distended or swollen belly as a child. Life was a tragedy wherein food was a major player. When my environment changed, so did my food. Now I ate poke weeds, also known as Phytolacca Americana (my-toe-LAK-ah am-er-i-KAY-na). Pokeweeds is a plant" that is poisonous if not prepared properly. Of course, as a child, I didn't know that this plant was dangerous. All I knew was that this toxic plant silenced the roaring sounds within my belly and responded to my innate need for survival. Later, I went from starch-fed to pokeweed, and now oatmeal-fed. Right from the start, oatmeal and I didn't get along. I struggled to swallow it without gagging this cold, lumpy, and slimy mess lying in my red tin bowl.

Sitting at the kitchen table, with my feet barely touching the floor, I endured stories about how oats were "good" for the horses, so it was good for me. Then, one day, I devised, at least to me, what I thought was an ingenious way to hide my oatmeal. Like a drug dealer hiding drugs, I stuffed my food in a plastic bag, transferred it to my schoolbook bag, and then threw the stash away in the front yard on my way to school. That's right, in the front yard, as if no one would find it.

Anyway, it didn't take long before I got caught. While sitting in school, my oatmeal surfaced in the front yard. When I arrived home, the verdict and sentencing rolled into one was swift and brutal. No appeal. No respite.; I paid for my sin with a beating. Even before I'd gone to confession, my penance was doled out. I hadn't counted on the oatmeal bag ever being discovered and retrieved. I suffered double— jeopardy for hiding the oatmeal and for not eating it. Years later, people told me that my dislike of oatmeal had to do with how it was cooked. It was too late; oatmeal was my first sworn enemy by then.

Evening meals consisted of beans with a slab of fatty meat, a dish known as pork and beans, which conflicted with my tastebuds and esophagus. My entrée was anger, misery, and unhappiness from the cook. It's important to note that I grew up on a poor menu, but that wasn't the problem. It was the misery that went with it, and not as a side dish. Over time I ate out of necessity, not enjoyment. And like most children, I dared not complain about my food.

I was often met with beatings for not eating my food, coupled with severe tongue lashings for throwing food away or wasting food. Back then, I couldn't even claim peanut, oat, grain, gluten allergies, or any of the sensitivities that are so common today. It wouldn't have mattered anyway. I was supposed to eat what was on my plate and eat all of it. I was constantly reminded of the children that did not have food, me being one of them. What I didn't eat in the morning, I had to eat in the evening, which brought on more gagging and plotting over that chaos on my plate.

Eating for me was a conditional exchange between existing and surviving. Life didn't factor into it except this one evening, I didn't feel well. I was about 7 or 8 years of age. I know I was in elementary school. By the time I came home, my body felt like fire, and I couldn't stand up. Sweating profusely and feeling weak, my small, frail body fell into the bed, lying motionless. Back then, emergency room was not an option unless you were dead. Death seemed imminent as it hovered over me. I remember being given herbs and a stern warning to get well by the morning for school. I think I was too scared to stay sick or even die. I'd never missed a day of school. When I woke up the the following day, I felt better and again face oatmeal on the table. After the front yard tragedy, I started outsourcing my oatmeal to my brothers in exchange for their cleaning duties or my allowance. I still didn't feel entirely well, but after the homemade tonics and rest, getting well was expected, while school was obligatory.

Fast forward to my adult years, when I could eat anything, I wanted. —I didn't know what to eat. Oddly, I still had this strange urge to eat corn starch and sometimes bought it to eat it secretly. When I think about it, no one talked about food except for its necessity for survival, or to compare having food with those that did not have it. Nonetheless, I'd grown unconscious, unmindful, and rebellious about what I was eating. Rebellious in the sense that I ate what I would never have been allowed to eat as a child, mainly junk. I can remember biting into my first tasty cake and someone telling me it was expired. Still, it tasted better than oatmeal. In looking back, I realize that sometimes, what was fed to me was not healthy. Nor did I like it. But when I gained control over what I ate, I may have enjoyed what I was eating, but that food was not good for me either.

My emotional struggle with food and ignorance in taking

care of myself was not in vain. Diagnosed with childhood arthritis, I went on with my life enduring my aches and pains and suffering from the damage of regurgitating my food from my teen years onward, along with residual anxiety. I couldn't keep food down, nor did I want to. Sometimes, I would go days without eating because I felt that not eating was the only thing in my power. Fainting and even finding an IV in my arm in the emergency room didn't deter me. This mindless and harmful eating way took its toll on me.

Indeed, illness is a master teacher. Malnourishment, anemia, autoimmune disorder, constipation, cancer, and witnessing several family members' deaths from diabetes and cardiovascular disease revealed that food was a force to be reckoned with- it could *kill or heal.* I embarked on a journey to become mindful of my food choices and the quality of my food. I invested in my health like others invest in stocks. You might say that not everyone can afford to eat healthily. To me, I say, I cannot afford to eat unhealthily. Consequently, I rearranged my life to make food quality and health my practices a priority line item, instead of television, cable, cellphones, fast foods, jewelry, vacations, shoes, clothes, cruises, sneakers, and social or even intimate relationships.

It's true; I ate in a highly charged emotional environment. Inside I carried this foreboding fear with me even when my environment changed, which made it difficult even to enjoy any food even though my environment had changed. That is until I understood my food story and committed to the healing process. When I did, I did not want my food fast; I wanted it nutritious. Like many people, where I ate didn't matter before my awakening, just as long as it wasn't too gross. However, after a while, I couldn't just eat anywhere. So I began to accommodate my new way of life by being particular about where I ate; if I did eat out, I wanted to know who was cooking my food. I familiarized myself with the owners and chefs of restaurants. Where we eat is just as important as what we eat. I also created a home environment infused with positive energy and wholesome nutrition to sustain my health. No longer did eating out excite me. Instead, I preferred home-cooking and began creating health on a plate or within a bowl, living by the mantra "Wellness Begins Inside."

From my direct experience, I learned the difference between eating mindlessly and eating mindfully. I saw a difference between meat-eating and adopting a plant-based diet, between low-quality foods and high-quality foods, and between eating out and at home. On my journey, I let go of meat and meat-based products and dairy products. It made sense that I prioritized what went into my body, not how many clothes accessorize my closet.

In full disclosure, I am a plant-based eater. Weighted down by cancer and other health concerns and having a family history loaded with mortalities, I refrained from consuming dairy, meat, and meat by-products. I've seen firsthand countless food-related deaths, the devastation of my family members, losing limbs and organs, and friends' and colleagues' early transitioning. It was heart-wrenching to see my brother on dialysis machines; I stood by as he lost both of his kidneys and mourned his predictable death. Unlike the doctors, who attributed his health challenges to genetics, I knew his food story, food addiction, life experiences, silent stresses, unresolved emotions, and the toxic environments we lived in, among other things. Regardless of the medical autopsy, I knew the actual cause of death was an unhappy childhood, a scarcity of nutritional food, unconscious eating, unresolved feelings, a low health quotient, and a failure to thrive.

In reflecting on my life, I gradually began understanding why I had no appetite; emotions, stress, and anxiety lingered in my mind and gut. My gut, sometimes referred to as the second brain, had seized up, and I didn't want to eat. I now know that I failed to thrive because of unresolved emotional challenges. Our brains and guts work in tandem, biologically and emotionally. For example, when stressed or nervous, I didn't want to eat. Others may have the opposite response and overeat during stressful periods. What is clear until we heal, our brains, our stomachs, and intestines will be at the mercy of our emotions.

I remember a woman I worked with every Tuesday; after being absent on Monday and Friday, she returned with a doctor's note excusing her absence due to gastrointestinal tract sensitivity. What the doctor didn't know that I knew, was that she didn't like the job, but her gut knew it.

My arduous but life-altering journey made it clear that we can be born into devastating circumstances, but as we grow, the choice is up to us how we live. How do you want to live? What we do to ourselves has a cumulative effect. Before you know it, we find ourselves carrying around a lifetime of unresolved emotions manifested through our eating. To counteract the inevitable damage, we must choose a wellness practice. We divorce our gastrointestinal doctors and sever ties with our disease alliance when we do. When I did, the wounds healed, and the medicine worked.

I connected with some master chefs, food artists, doctors, and connoisseurs who ignited a fire to create healthy, beautiful cuisines for myself and others. With commitment, constant study, research, and practice, I became inspired by food's inherent healing power gradually flowing from within to emerge as a path for healing. Finally, I no longer ate fearfully, rebelliously, or for survival, but joyfully, mindfully, and nutritiously. So, what is your food story?

What is your food story?

WHY

Nothing can survive without food, including happiness; your happiness can die if you do not know how to nourish it.
-Thich Nhat Hanh

Why do we eat? It sounds like an uncomplicated question, but is it? We most likely respond, "Because we're hungry," right? But what does it mean to be hungry? Even if we eat because we're hungry, what does that mean? *Actual* hunger is a highly complex process that cues our body to need fuel or energy. When we're hungry, a message is processed and sent through the "gray matter of our brains, which mainly makes up 40 percent% of the brain's surface or outer cerebral cortex. Our gray matter is a vital part of the central nervous system. It extends to the spinal cord and accounts for most of the brain's neuronal cell bodies, which manage information processing and this sensation of hunger. During the processing of hunger, our brain triggers either a hormone that signals us to eat or one for us to stop eating.

The hormone called ghrelin, "the hunger" hormone gets a message from nerves in the stomach that tells us we're hungry. These two hormones reside in the stomach, coordinating our food intake activity. Our grey matter then receives this hunger message from our guts that it's time to fuel up, so we eat. A grocery store opens in our heads, causing us to respond to our hunger needs by looking for something to eat. It doesn't tell us what to eat. Instead, we eat what we like, whether oatmeal or eggs, cheesesteak or salad; ice cream or an apple; mac and cheese, jelly doughnut or nuts, a large white pizza, or a bowl of navy bean soup. After eating, the hunger alarm should turn off after providing fuel for about two to three hours. We eat in response to the low-fuel messaging from our stomachs, which we fill until a feeling of fullness occurs again.

Our feeling of hunger is not a forever-on device. At least, it shouldn't be. If all systems are operating correctly, we have an automatic shut-off valve to signal fullness or enough to eat gauge. Fullness is under the control of the leptin hormone. Leptin is often referred to as the "satiety hormone." When leptin comes on duty, this hormone tells our brains that we don't need to eat anymore and decreases our appetite because enough fat is stored to burn calories at an average rate. As the saying goes, we have dined sufficiently. So, it's time to stop eating.

This ghrelin and leptin interaction sounds relatively routine, but there is a catch. The message of fullness is not instant and can take between 15-20 minutes after our first bites to reach our brain. We could still be eating even though we're technically full by that time. We call this overeating going beyond what the body needs. Have you ever overfilled your gas tank? What happens is the gas spills out on the ground. We should wait before we go for the second serving because it allows for the activation of fullness to kick in.

We bypass the ghrelin hormones and deactivate the leptin hormones when we overeat. Every day, many of us are doing just that. Why do we do that? Are we hungry, bored, upset, or anxious? Are we entertaining ourselves to death with the wrong foods? Perhaps we're not even eating food, so we're not full. With so many food ads, billboards, and stimuli around us, especially all-you-can-eat buffets- we eat all that we see, not what we need, ignoring the food stop sign by disabling the Leptin hormone. When we override these circuitries, this causes malfunctioning of our Ghrelin and Leptin hormones, the natural processing of hunger and fullness.

Hunger, however, is just not about hormones and this sensation of fullness. Eating is also tied to our autonomic nervous system: the sympathetic nervous system (SNS), commonly known as the fight-or-flight or stress response center, and the parasympathetic nervous system (PNS), often referred to as the rest-and-digest response center or relaxation response center. The vagus nerves, the longest nerve in the human body, originate in the brain and interact with the heart, lungs, spleen, gallbladder, kidneys, and digestive tract. Imagine the body as a major corporation; the vagus nerves are the chief executive headquartered within the parasympathetic or relaxation department. Their duties include managing heart rate, gastrointestinal issues, and muscle movements in the mouth, including swallowing and speech, and sustaining overall balance. Even though we may be unfamiliar with vagus nerves, as we can see, these nerves sustain our lives.

Stress response leads to stress eating. When we feel excessively overwhelmed, stress depletes the vagus nerves and inhibits our relaxation ability. When that happens, we activate our stress response which triggers us to eat more often and more of the wrong foods, leading us down that path of chronic diseases, such as being overweight or underweight, type 2 diabetes, heart attacks, strokes, and many other health problems.

With our vagus nerves rendered temporarily inactive, the snooze button is depressed for the parasympathetic nervous system or our relaxation response. Who thinks about eating healthy when they're stressed? The good news is that we can tone our vagus nerves and activate our parasympathetic nervous systems for relaxation rather than stress-eating. Stress response incites us to eat even though we are actually hungry.

Why do we eat? Let's count the reasons-our grey gray matter, the two hormones, the autonomic and central nervous center, and the vagus nerves. But there are other reasons we eat, for one, social. How often do we eat out with friends and the family simply because they asked? Or perhaps someone calls, so we go out just to eat? Interestingly, research has noted the following benefits of eating with others: it's enjoyable and makes us feel good. As well, social eating supposedly fosters a higher self-confidence, and it helps us the attainment of a more extensive social group.

In contrast, our social appetite can also result in social eating. That is, eating when we're not hungry, but for the social reward of being around others. And so, for some, the downside to social eating is overeating or the disregarding the leptin hormones telling us we're full and to move away from the table. Still, communal eating increases social bonding and feelings of well-being. In the United States, thousands of restaurants exist ready to facilitate that bonding. It's not just the food but the social reinforcement that goes along with eating out with others. Yet, the positive reinforcement of being socially connected around others or social connectivity increases our eating. With social groupings as the reward, we overeat.

So, if social eating is communally reinforcing, what is emotional eating? One word: *"Feelings."* With emotional eating, we consume large quantities of food, usually "comfort" or junk food, in response to feelings instead of true hunger. Social eating is external and group-oriented, while emotional eating is internal and may happen with or without a group. Some experts estimate that 75% percent of overeating is caused by our emotions again overriding the leptin, or fullness hormones so that we go straight through the red light and eat more. That means we sometimes eat when we're not hungry but to relieve discomfort or stress relief, and even self-reward ourselves, among other such reasons. We convince ourselves that we deserve it. We reach for junk food, sweets, and other comforting but unhealthy foods when that happens. We might order a pizza or eat cookies or ice cream to respond to the stress in our lives. With emotional eating, we use food as therapy or as a pacifier. Of course, emotional eating is unhealthy and has several adverse side effects, such as weight gain and overeating. Other side effects of emotional eating include guilt, stubbornness, difficulty treating hard-to-treat depression, or other mental health problems.

Usually, when we talk about emotional eating, overweight monopolizes the conversation, rarely do we consider that some people's appetite becomes suppressed. Thus, they are reluctant to eat for emotional reasons. The reason may be, for example, a fear of gaining weight or and for others, a failure to thrive. One of my family members recently died with "the failure to thrive" notation diagnosis on his medical charts. He weighed less than seventy pounds at eighty years old and had stopped eating when his mother died. But no one noticed. His appearance was that of someone starving to death. Although his doctors encouraged him to eat, he didn't. That concept of failure to thrive lingered with me because it speaks to the psychological challenge of living with grief, trauma, unresolved childhood emotions, and life's uncertainties. He was starving to death, not because of the lack of food but because of an unwillingness to eat. What do we do with our traumatic experiences threatening our vitality? Do we succumb to the threat by losing our appetite for life, or do we mindfully eat to live meaningful lives?

When I was younger, I could go days without eating or only minimally eating, which led to fainting and overall weakness. While non--eaters are on the opposite end of the spectrum from overeaters, it's still unhealthy. Just because you're skinny doesn't mean you're healthy. The term *"skinny fat"* refers to someone who looks healthy by weight standards but carries too much body fat and insufficient muscle mass: *skinny fat*. Skinny-fat individuals can suffer from metabolic problems like nutritional deficiencies, high cholesterol elevations, and even hypertension. Whether the conditions are of being overweight, underweight or skinny fat, they're all signals of health risks and emotional concerns.

Emotional eating goes unnoticed because habitual eating is the norm. Our sadness, grief, disappointment, anger, hurt, and other emotions get ignored. I met a woman who admitted that her weight was due to several life stressors, such as loss of job loss and a relationship breakup. She lamented that she would lose weight and gain it back again. It was the eating that captured my attention. Most of her story centered around her heartbreak from a romantic relationship that she had expected to lead to marriage. Another person shared that she ate the way she did because they weren't in a relationship and wanted to be in one; she substituted food for intimacy. Still, another individual attended participated in a popular weight program wherein she would lose 5 pounds and feel good and then gain 10 ten lbs pounds and feel depressed.

This losing and gaining all had to do with how she felt at that particular moment. But like a child who received a star for good behavior, she proudly wore her weight loss sticker near her right shoulder, displaying her temporary success. Often, we aren't conscious of our *weight gain*, but we are unconscious of the weight gained. We aren't aware that much of our excess weight appears to be symptomatic of our unconscious, unresolved emotional issues from our childhoods. Still, too much and too little weight represents our food story and unresolved emotions.

Is there more to why we eat other than physical, social, and emotional? An outside force encourages us to eat- it's called the environment. Yes, there is. For example, when we're at work, we may eat even though we're full because our work situations call for us to eat again. Rather than create an uncomfortable environment, we eat to maintain camaraderie and harmony with our co-workers. And so, some of our weight gain and metabolic imbalances may be attributable to the workplace. Eating is environmentally triggered. How often have you gone out with your co-workers for Happy Hour drinks and cheese fries or a Long Island iced tea and Chicken Wings with our co-workers?

We eat not because we're hungry but because it's there. Eating environments like this are called "obesogenic," a term coined by Boyd Swinburn, a public health expert from New Zealand(Pincock 2011), over 25 twenty-five years ago. Swinburn observed the adverse impacts of high diabetes rates on the Native Americans at a reservation in Arizona. From his research, he found out that obesogenic environments, home or workplace, encourage weight gain while hindering weight loss. The workplace weight gain is a reality, with breaks consisting of eating; and food carts filled with limitless unhealthy snacks.

Some of the attributes of obesogenic environments include proximal eating, which is associated with the distance between you and food. In our current home environments, due to the coronavirus, we're eating more not only because of stress but our proximity and access to food. And so, weight-gaining environments include proximity eating; Food is close by and ever-present.

Another insight is that exercise such as walking, and jogging, especially in specific neighborhoods, is uncommon. In addition, children used to play outside, run, and engage in outdoor play games. No more. Children in crime-dense communities often are kept inside for safety reasons. More and more, these children are not allowed out to play because of the danger. Too often to mention, parents have shared with me their fear of letting their children go outside because of violence, which leads them to restrict their children to the indoors, where they occupy themselves inside with an iPad, video games, or television. That's a reality for too many children. It's no wonder that the obesity rate in children continues to grow. Data from the State of Childhood Obesity indicate that during the pandemic, the national rate of obesity among children ages 2 to 19 increased to 22.4% in 2020. Whether referring to children or adults, living at home or work, being in an obesogenic environment is not exclusive to the inner city. Any environment that promotes obesity rather than healthy eating habits is obesogenic.

Look around your environment? Are you living an obesogenic lifestyle? Is it a sedentary or an active lifestyle? When was the last time you took a walk or exercised? Does your environment encourage unhealthiness through overeating, a caloric-heavy diet, and a lack of physical activity? Although we didn't talk about it, some cultures encourage repeated eating under the guise of culture. If so, for the sake of your health and healing-change is imperative.

With everything we've discussed, what do we mean when we say we're hungry? Two types of hunger exist: One is homeostatic or natural hunger, which balances our energy reserves. And the other is hedonic or pleasure hunger, and it is the breeding ground that leads us to gather extra, albeit unnecessary, energy and fat. This happens when we're eating on a full stomach, for pleasure or hedonic reasons. Along with other physiological responses, our heart rates, blood sugar, blood pressure, and cholesterol levels rise. Thus, pleasure eating does come with a cost. And it results — not only in the metabolic imbalances but also in consuming excessive calories. Pleasure eating motivates our hunger for things aside from survival, such as social, recreational, emotional, and environmental reasons.

Why we *should* eat may not be *why* we *do* eat. Our reasons for overeating are mixed. Some of us eat primarily to be healthy, and others for social, pleasurable, recreational, emotional, and even environmental reasons. In these modern times, when we are surrounded by all-night eateries, fast food, food courts, food carts, street food, food on the go, and so on, our eating may be less about survival or even balance and more about pleasure. Whatever is behind our eating, a story exists. We must ask ourselves these questions: Are we eating because we're hungry? Or because we are unhappy? Is eating something to do (STDs)? Are we feeding our bodies, experiences, emotions, or environments to the detriment of our life? Is something eating us? In *Wellness Begins Inside,* we eat to heal.

Awareness: Why do you eat?

	Often	Sometimes	Rarely
Because I'm hungry			
Because I'm stressed			
Because I'm angry			
Because I'm bored			
Because I'm lonely			
Because I'm pressured			
Other Reasons			

WHAT

The secret to living well and longer is eat half, walk double, laugh triple, and love without measure.—Tibetan Proverb

Now that we know why we eat, let's turn our attention to what we're eating. What are you eating right now? An apple, a cheesesteak, fries, donuts, candy, or a salad? According to the data, it's more than likely that it's takeout, and it's probably chicken wings or pizza. French fries, potato chips, snack foods, pizzas, burgers, hotdogs, chili, and cheesecakes are enjoyed by a lot of us. Pizza tops as the favorite foods, with chicken wings being amongst our favorites. Food has become synonymous with fast food chain names. Often when I asked children to name foods, they name places like McDonald's, Wendy's, or Chick-fil-a; a few will name foods such as French fries, chicken, pizza, and mac and cheese. Places have replaced the actual names of foods. Together with our fast-food addiction, our preference for sweetness has grown threefold. Soft drinks are becoming America's favorite breakfast beverage, consumed alongside specialty sandwiches and breakfast burritos. If we take a closer look at what we like, we can see that it boils down to crunchy, salty, and sweet.

Our sweet tongue is insatiable, but where did it come from? According to Willett et al. *Eat, drink and be healthy: The Harvard Medical School Guide to healthy eating*, "we probably evolved our sense of sweetness to detect subtle amounts of carbohydrates in foods because they provide energy." … "but now the expectations of sweetness have been ratcheted up. A product is not attractive if it is not as sweet as its competitor."

And so, we drink sugar coffee and tea. Just look at the nutrition facts label on the back of your food; you'll see the total sugar in a serving measured in grams as well how much of that is added sugar. If a product contains 0.6 grams of sugar and 0.55 grams of that is added sugar, is that too much? Recently, a friend of mine ordered a bottled iced tea and, upon looking at the nutrition facts label, discovered that it had a whopping 46 grams of sugar, and 91 percent of that was added sugar. Sweetness has become our weakness and an acceptable drug of choice. It comes to us in two ways: hidden and upfront. Today, sugar *added* to foods makes up 16 percent of the calories in our diets.

But whether it's sweet stuff, fried chicken, or cheesy pizza, what we eat falls into two definite fuel categories: nutritious and poisonous. Fuel provides power and energy so we can go about our daily activities. Yet not all fuel is the same. For example, you wouldn't put diesel fuel in a car that takes only gas. Why? It would damage the vehicle.

Similarly, putting the wrong fuel in our bodies will harm us, because the body processes it as poison. Unfortunately, the fuel we've grown accustomed to using today may be poison. One of the most dangerous assumptions I made early on in my life was that whatever stores sold as food was food. Later, I would learn that some of the things we even buy from the grocery store may be food-like but are not actually food. Mistakenly we assume that those things are keeping us alive, where in actuality, they may be causing diseases and hastening our deaths. This brings us to the question, What does the body need for optimal health?

Countless health experts from various walks of life bombard us with conflicting information about what to eat, what not to eat, when to eat, and even what supplements we need to buy (exclusively from them). Some say to eliminate rice or apples, tomatoes or wheat, dairy or protein; some try to free us of lectins, carbohydrate-binding proteins found in all plants and animals. Others tell us to eat only raw food, which means nothing heated over 104–118°F, or to eat clean, which means home-cooked, organic, unprocessed, whole grains and seasonal fruits. Eating has come down to a blue-book test. But what are the actual facts?

Mindlessly eating is the culprit. Without thinking about nutrition facts, like the 91 percent added sugar in the iced tea, we drink it. We often forget what we even ate. Or eat what we feel like, not what's necessarily healthy. I know I did. I just ate, oblivious to what type of fuel my body required. Besides, I was unaware of the inner workings of my body. I left it up to doctors to tell me when parts of my body were malfunctioning. You'd think that we'd treat our most valuable assets better, yet rarely do we consider the effects of food on our bodies. Take carbs. We usually hear about them when someone is trying to lose weight, but do we understand the functional nature of carbs as it pertains to our health? For me, as long as my blood work came back okay, I was fine. I didn't connect the type or quality of my food to my blood work. What about those occasional conversations we have about protein, which I thought pertained mainly to athletes or bodybuilders? Protein didn't mean too much to me. Sure, I walked and occasionally ran, but not to the point that protein crossed my mind.

In this age of social media, so much is put out there as science regarding food. It becomes confusing. We hear "don't eat this," and we stop, not understanding the complete picture. Our eating resembles a game of Whack-a-Mole, where we whack the foods as they pop up. No one teaches us life-sustaining nutrition, which for many remains a mystery. We eat what we ate.

So, adults pass down to their children not only their unhealthy food choices but their disease susceptibilities. When we get older, sometimes we're so far gone eating a certain way that it's difficult for us to change. Our harmful lifestyles have become addictive. My brother was like that; he ate all he could eat and ate whatever, primarily salty and sweet things. Even when his body started to break down like a car that needed a new engine, carburetor, and transmission and new brakes, he kept eating the same way. It was nothing for me to visit him and see a stack of pancakes with three or four eggs and extra bacon on the side.

Fortunately for me, I was drawn toward a completely different path. My family history, a litter of dead siblings, deceased parents, my bout with cancers, and my autoimmune disorder scared me straight. I was awakened. Suffering from constipation, bloating, and even cancer, I treated myself like a food lab. But unlike Morgan Spurlock, in the documentary *Super-Size Me*, I choose to eat healthy. Rather than let my DNA determine my destiny, I aligned myself with epigenetic science, which speaks to what we do to express our genes. Besides, I would have been dead in a month, subjecting my body to the way Spurlock ate.

Instead, I wondered if there would be a difference in my genetic history and metabolic panels if I ate differently from my family. So, I embarked on this journey to live a different life than I saw my family living. Too often, as African-Americans, we often hear statements of hopelessness at the doctor's office, as if we're destined to be obese and suffer from high blood pressure, cardiovascular disease, and diabetes, when we're cursed by low health expectations. But while that's the expectation, it doesn't have to be the reality. We know doctors only prescribe more and more pills, rarely asking about the foods we eat. I wanted to change that message of hopelessness to hopefulness by exploring what we should be putting inside our bodies, fads aside, to turn off the genetic expression; I wanted to become mindful of what I might be doing to express diseases by finding out what did the body need.

This is what I found out; we should be consuming a highly calibrated group of essential nutrients. These six essential nutrients, the best fuel for the body, are *carbohydrates, protein*, *fat*, *vitamins*, *minerals*, and *wat*er. But there is a seventh nutrient I discovered that's often overlooked, and that is *love*. For me, love is essential not only in eating but also in cooking. Love is when our food becomes an instrument of healing. All of these nutrients are macronutrients. We need to know three things about macronutrients: they make up most of our diet, they *cannot* be produced by our bodies, and they come from what we eat. Vitamins and minerals, on the other hand, are micronutrients. We need them but in smaller amounts. So, macronutrients we need more, and micronutrients we need less. Let's explore the inner nutritional requisite of the body.

Macronutrients

Carbohydrates

Carbohydrates are the most common and abundant forms of sugars, fiber, and starches found in the body. Sugar, or glucose is reserved for energy. Fiber is critical in keeping the digestive system well-tuned. Starch, another essential energy source contains B vitamins, iron, calcium, and folate.

Good or Complex Carbs

Complex carbs are unprocessed or minimally processed. "Your body needs to break down complex carbohydrates because they're a complicated mesh of molecules," says Lauren Harris-Pincus, M.S., R.D.N., and owner of Nutrition Starring. Apparently, these carbs are *good* because they provide most of our energy and a lasting and stable energy elevation. It takes the body longer to break down complex carbs, and they also provide micronutrients such as vitamins and minerals our body needs. Examples of good carbs include vegetables, fruit, pulses, legumes, beans, sweet potatoes, unsweetened dairy products, and whole grains, like brown rice, air-popped popcorn, quinoa, wheat, and oats.

Bad or Refined Carbs

The term *bad carbs* is plain. These refined carbohydrates possess little fiber and are composed of refined sugar and starches. Refined carbs are easily and quickly digested and contribute to diabetes, elevated blood pressure, heart diseases, and difficulty losing weight. In addition, these carbs have a high glycemic index, which causes an unhealthy spike in blood sugar levels. They're devoid of fiber and nutrients.

Since diabetes runs in my family, this information, for me, became a way not to pass diabetes to another generation. By changing the type of carbs I was eating, I could decrease my likelihood of developing diabetes, among other diseases.

Examples of diabetes-triggering foods include pizza dough, white bread, those innocent looking pastries at your favorite coffee shop, cakes, sweet desserts, pasta, white (processed) rice, breakfast cereals, cookies, and other bakery items made with white flour. But of course, we rarely ask for an order of unhealthy carbs. We merely order pizza, pretzels, doughnuts, bread, or a side of potatoes; or our favorite sweet coffee and bad carbs as if it's not going to affect us.

We all eat carbs in our everyday life. And even though some people follow a low-carb diet, our carb intake should be healthy and nutritionally rich, rather than being composed of unhealthy carbs that are nutritionally empty of minerals, vitamins, and enzymes and lead to many diseases and illnesses, such as obesity, high cholesterol, and even depression.

Knowing that carbs are essential for fuel and energy, what types of carbs will you choose going forth? Will you consume too many carbs in one sitting or consider a low-carb diet where you obtain only 30 to 40 percent of your calories from carbs? What type of carbs will you choose, good or bad? Old habits do die hard, but with determination we can make them a habit of the past, and *Wellness Begins Inside*.

Protein (Macronutrient)

Humans do not live by carbs alone. Protein is essential for building muscle mass, cartilage, bones, skin, hair, and nails. We have amino acids, hormones, and enzymes that are hard at work ensuring that our bodies are properly functioning. Amino acids (derived from protein) are not something we talk about, but they are essential to our health. There are twenty-one amino acids, or chemical compounds, of which nine have been designated essential for us to grow and function.

Usually, we don't see amino acids listed on the nutrition facts label, but we see protein.

Complete proteins are foods that contain all nine essential amino acids: histidine, isoleucine, leucine, lysine, methionine, phenylalanine, threonine, tryptophan, and valine. These amino acids are like power packs that provide us with a sense of equanimity by regulating blood, immune function, digestion, libido, sleep, fat metabolism, muscle growth, and even wound healing.

One that caught my attention was tryptophan, because of its connection to serotonin, a neurotransmitter that regulates our appetites, sleep, and moods. Tryptophan is needed to produce serotonin, a chemical that acts as a neurotransmitter in your body. Serotonin is our feel-good neurotransmitter that, when low, affects mood, sleep, and behavior. Of course, no one goes around talking about low tryptophan or even serotonin, but what if our low serotonin levels come from low amounts of amino acids, which must come from our food sources or supplements? Could our moods and behaviors be linked to amino acid deficiencies?

Sources of complete proteins include meats, milk, fish, eggs, and plant sources such as soy, grains, and quinoa. Beans, legumes, and nuts are incomplete proteins. Therefore, when we eat complete proteins, such as grain and other plant sources, we can meet our essential amino acid needs without choosing animal products.

"When protein is broken down in the body, it helps to fuel muscle mass, which helps metabolism," says Jessica Crandall, a registered dietitian nutritionist, certified diabetes educator, and national spokesperson for the Academy of Nutrition and Dietetics. "It also helps the immune system stay strong. It helps you stay full. A lot of research has shown that protein has satiety effects." As such, protein also plays a role in reducing our tendency to overeat.

Since I am a vegetarian, the question always arises as to whether I'm getting enough protein. It turns out that we don't need as much protein as we think. Besides, high-protein diets can carry some health risks. Too much of a good thing can be harmful. According to the Mayo Clinic, excessive consumption of protein reduces carbohydrate intake, leading to nutritional and fiber deficiencies. Eating too much protein can also cause headaches, constipation, increased risk of heart disease, and, worse, kidney malfunctions in those suffering from kidney disease.

"There's a growing body of research that suggests that Americans are getting enough protein," Jessica Crandall says. Again, it is recommended that we split our protein so that we get enough protein at each meal. For example, protein should be consumed within an hour of waking up, then every four to six hours after that.

Fat

We've heard the saying "that's phat," meaning cool or great, but not all fat is cool. Still, fat is necessary. Our body needs some fat from food. What is it that fat does? There are five benefits from fat: it (1) absorbs some vitamins and minerals; (2) supports cell growth; (3) builds cell membranes, the vital exterior of each cell; (4) builds the sheath surrounding nerves; and (5) is essential for blood clotting, muscle movement, and inflammation. Fat provides us with energy. However, some fats are better than others.

Similar to carbs, we have good and bad fats. Unsaturated fats, such as monounsaturated and polyunsaturated fats, are good, industrial-made trans fats are bad, and saturated fats fall somewhere in the middle. So first, let's explore some fats.

Unsaturated Fats

Unsaturated fats become liquefied at room temperature, are considered to be beneficial because they improve blood cholesterol levels, ease inflammation, stabilize heart rhythms, and play several other valuable roles. We find unsaturated fats in foods derived from plants, such as vegetable oils, nuts, and seeds. There are two types of "good" unsaturated fats: monounsaturated and polyunsaturated.

Monounsaturated fats are found in high concentrations in

- olive, peanut, and canola oils.
- avocados
- nuts such as almonds, hazelnuts, and pecans; and
- seeds such as pumpkin and sesame seeds.

Polyunsaturated fats are found in high concentrations in

- sunflower, corn, soybean, and flaxseed oils.
- walnuts
- flax seeds
- fish.

Canola oil, though higher in monounsaturated fat, is considered a good source of polyunsaturated fat.

Omega-3 fatty acids are an essential type of polyunsaturated fat. That means the body can't make these, so they must come from food. Omega-3s may help prevent and even treat heart disease and strokes. In addition to reducing blood pressure, raising HDL cholesterol, and lowering triglycerides, polyunsaturated fats may help prevent lethal heart rhythms from arising. Evidence also suggests they may help reduce the need for corticosteroid medications in people with rheumatoid arthritis. An excellent way to get omega-3 fatty acids is by eating fish two to three times a week. Good plant sources of omega-3s include flax seeds, walnuts, canola oil, and soybean oil.

Saturated Fats

Saturated fats are common in the American diet. But how do we determine the amount of saturated fat that is acceptable? In *the Sinister S's,* we'll delve deeper into the usefulness or uselessness of saturated fat. But for now, the consensus is that we should limit the amount of saturated fat in our diet.

Trans Fats

Unanimously, the jury has found trans fats to be the most dangerous type of dietary fat, which clogs our arteries. Trans fats are the byproduct of a hydrogenation process used to turn healthy oils into solids. They have no known health benefits; neither is there a safe level of consumption. For that reason, in 2015 the US Food and Drug Administration (FDA) officially banned the use of trans fats, or partially hydrogenated oils, in all foods sold in American restaurants and grocery stores because of its link to heart attacks.

Caution is advised because we may still be consuming trans fats, especially if we travel. Also, knowing the trans-fat content of the food we consume is unlikely if we eat most of our meals outside of the home. What's more, we can't always determine the amount of trans fat in a particular packaged food by looking at the nutrition facts. Some products will say they contain "0 grams of trans fat," but that only means they contain less than 0.5 grams of trans fat per serving. Hence, we identify trans-fat content by reading ingredient lists and looking for the ingredients referred to as "partially hydrogenated oils."

I couldn't help thinking about the years I and others have unknowingly consumed trans fats before its legal exclusion from our diets. I thought that what is legal may not always be what is healthy, and we shouldn't have to wait for laws to be passed to take charge of our health. Government is not responsible for taking care of us.

Undeniably, eating foods with trans fats increases harmful LDL cholesterol in the bloodstream and reduces beneficial HDL cholesterol. In addition, trans fats create inflammation linked to heart disease, stroke, diabetes, and other chronic conditions. They also contribute to insulin resistance, which increases the risk of developing type 2 diabetes. Trans fats are like a one-two punch to the gut, increasing harmful cholesterol while decreasing healthy cholesterol. It's a health hazard. I saw its effect firsthand after the deaths of several of my family members.

Examples of foods containing trans fats include fried foods, like doughnuts; baked goods, like cakes, pie crusts, biscuits, and cookies; frozen pizza; crackers; and stick margarine. If you're eating these foods, transition away from them. Do you know how much fat is inside that sweet beverage you drink every morning? Check it out?

How many carbs, proteins, and fats do we need?

Now that we have some information about what we need, the next question is, how much? According to nutritional guidelines, if we consume 2,000 calories a day, between 900 and 1,300 calories should come from good/complex carbohydrates. That translates into between 225 and 325 grams or 1.37 cups of carbohydrates a day. According to the Dietary Guidelines for Americans, carbohydrates should make up 45 to 65 percent of our total daily calories.

Nutritional Guidelines say that a daily protein intake of 1.6–2.2 grams of protein per kilogram of body weight (0.73–1.0 grams per pound) is sufficient for average people to lose weight. For athletes and heavy exercisers, that number should come to 2.2–3.4 grams of protein per kilogram (1.0–1.5 grams per pound) if they are aiming for weight loss.

In reviewing nutrition fact labels, I saw something was missing: starch, a complex carbohydrate, is not on the labels. After some searching, I found out that starch content doesn't have to be listed, only the total carbohydrates. Don't worry. We can calculate the starch grams by subtracting the number of grams of fiber and sugar from the total amount of carbohydrates; the remainder equals the number of grams of starch in that food serving. For example, brown rice has 33 grams of carbs. If we subtract the 2 grams of fiber and 1 gram of sugar it contains, we're left with 30 grams of starch. Is that a too much, too little or an adequate about of starch? An adequate intake of starch should be between 100 and 278 grams a day, based on a 1,600- to 2,200-calorie diet.

Although starch content is unlisted on the nutritional facts label, excessively refined starch is connected to a higher risk of diabetes, heart disease, and weight gain. High starch levels cause our blood sugar to spike rapidly. And so, if we're diagnosed with diabetes or prediabetes, we should be aware of our starch consumption; they cause blood glucose levels to rise. Three facts are clear: you should eat foods with less refined starch; you should consume healthy starches, like -vegetables, whole grains, beans, legumes, and fruit; and finally, you should reduce the portion of starches on a plate. Examples of starchy foods include corn, rice, potatoes, pasta, and white bread with 1/3-cup serving of pasta equaling nearly 15 grams of starch.

We have a dietary reference intake for fat as well. For adults, fats should account for 20 to 35 percent of their daily calories. That is about 44 to 77 grams or ¾ cup of fat per day based on a diet of 2,000 calorie a day

To sum up, protein, fats, and carbs, which include sugars, starches, and fiber, enrich our health and provide us with the opportunity to fulfill our purpose when consumed mindfully. Indeed, they are our medicine, but if used wrongly become our poison.

Micronutrients

Vitamins

According to a recent online survey conducted by the Harris Poll on behalf of the American Osteopathic Association, 86 percent of Americans take vitamin supplements. Go into many homes, and you'll find a random selection of vitamins. Walk into most stores, you'll find an entire aisle reserved for vitamins

Why do we take them? For the same reason we eat—to stay alive, to have longevity, and to be healthy. But do vitamins really work? Let's count the ways: They help us resist infections, keep our nerves healthy, help the body grow, acquire energy from food, and even help blood to clot properly. Unfortunately, most of us do not know our deficiencies and haphazardly take the most popular vitamins, such as B, C, D, and E. Our bodies require thirteen vitamins: A, C, D, E, K, and the B vitamins (thiamine, riboflavin, niacin, pantothenic acid, biotin, B6, B12, and folate). Of all the vitamins, K is the one we're least familiar with, yet vitamin K is needed for blood clotting, wound healing, and bone health. A good food source for vitamin K leafy greens, such as kale, spinach, turnip greens, collards, Swiss chard, mustard greens, parsley, romaine, and green leaf lettuce.

Did you know our bodies make vitamins D and K or that foods like fruits and vegetables, whole grains, beans and legumes, low-fat protein, and dairy products provide most of our vitamins? Other vitamin-rich everyday foods include eggs, nuts, bananas, broccoli, and cauliflower, which is filled with vitamin B6. Vitamins are also abundant in carrots, apricots, squash, red peppers, mango, and sweet potatoes.

The problem is that many of us are not eating enough vitamin- and mineral-enriched foods. As a result, we're both malnourished and vitamin deficient. That's why, supplements become necessary. Today's common micronutrient deficiencies include vitamins *B, C, D, and E, iodine, magnesium, and molybdenum*. Even plant-based eaters may have to supplement their diets with vitamins B12 and D3 (cholecalciferol), creatine, docosahexaenoic acid (DHA), heme iron, and taurine, which is an amino acid found in meat and fish that is used by our muscles, tissues, and brains and regulates calcium levels.

Needless to say, these deficiencies lead to health problems. For example, if you don't get enough vitamin B-12 and vitamin C, you could become anemic, a condition where your hemoglobin is low. When I was younger, I suffered from anemia and was placed on an iron supplement called Feosol. With anemia, I fainted often and felt tired and weak. As I've got older, a vitamin D deficiency also surfaced, so I started taking a lanolin-free, food-sourced D3 50 mcg (2000IU) vitamin supplement. I didn't feel any symptoms from the vitamin D deficiency, but I learned that low levels of this vitamin can result in bone and joint pain and tiredness. Last lab result revealed no vitamin D deficiencies. Most of us are unaware of the deficiencies within our bodies until we become ill. We don't realize that some vitamins may go so far as to prevent medical problems. Vitamin A, for instance, helps prevent night blindness, and if we are deficient, taking vitamin D, high-dose vitamin C, zinc, and potassium may help strengthen our immune systems—and their ability to help in fighting the virus responsible for the recent pandemic.

We love our vitamins. The amount of money spent on vitamins globally is around $82 billion a year, with roughly 28 percent of that being spent in the US. Even though vitamins sound harmless, we have to be careful. Close to six thousand companies pump out about seventy-five thousand products that may be unsuitable for us. That's right, some supplements have been known to be harmful. Of course, the optimal way to get enough vitamins is to eat a balanced diet with various foods, but because many of us do not, vitamin supplements become an alternative. Always check in with a health care provider with any concerns about your health.

According to the dietary reference intakes, 92 percent of the population suffers from at least one mineral or vitamin deficiency. Apparently, half of Americans suffer from deficiencies in vitamins A, C, and D, regardless of age. However, interestingly, vitamin A and vitamin C content are no longer required by the FDA to be listed on the nutrition facts label. Instead, they've been replaced with vitamin D and potassium levels. The reasoning behind this decision from our health department is that nowadays, A and C deficiencies are uncommon and thus no longer a concern. According to the Cooper Institute, 70 to 90 percent of Americans of color have vitamin D deficiencies. If you look closely at your nutrition facts labels, there is a section for the vitamin content on the bottom. Warning too much of anything is not good, and that includes mega doses of some vitamins. Vitamins A, D, E, K, B-3, B-6, B-9, and B-12 all have toxicity levels. Make an appointment with your health care professional to find out what your body needs before you start randomly ingesting vitamins.

Minerals

Another kind of micronutrient is macrominerals, such as calcium, zinc, iron, and potassium. *Macro* means "large," and so they are required in our diets in relatively large amounts. They're essential to the optimal functioning of the body. For example, we know our cells need a sodium-to-potassium ratio of one to three, which means our potassium intake would ideally be around three times our sodium intake. This ratio is vital to our health. Sodium and potassium are minerals.

Along with vitamins, mineral supplements support the systems within our bodies, but the best, most naturally usable sources of minerals are again foods. From promoting healthy bones and teeth to maintaining the integrity of bodily functions, like energy production, immune health, and nerve and muscle function, minerals go a long way to keeping your body functioning and healthy. We obtain our mineral quotient by eating plants that absorb them from rocks and soils or eating meat from animals that eat plants. In addition, minerals are essential for cell function.

Microminerals, like iodine and fluoride, are only needed in minimal quantities, unlike macrominerals, like calcium, magnesium, and potassium, of which more massive amounts are necessary. For example, sometimes magnesium is administered intravenously in the emergency room to help maintain normal heart rhythms, reducing the risk of cardiac arrythmia, an irregular, often rapid heartbeat that obstructs blood flow.

As with vitamins, if we eat a wholesome diet, we will probably get enough minerals. The fifteen foods highest in mineral content are nuts, beans and lentils, dark leafy greens, fish, seeds, mushrooms, avocados, tofu, dark chocolate, and dried fruit and whole grains. If you eat meat or fish, its shellfish, low-fat dairy, beef and lamb, and cheese. Again, we must ask ourselves “Are we eating a diet enrich with vitamins and minerals”?

Water

We do not live by vitamins or minerals alone; we need water. Every cell, tissue, and organ in your body requires water to work correctly. Water maintains our temperature, removes waste, and lubricates our joints. Water is essential in sustaining our health, but it’s so often an afterthought. Even doctors will ask, are you drinking water? Water is medicinal.

You’d think that being composed of 60 percent water or fluids, we’d drink more. Water supports digestion, absorption, circulation, saliva creation, transportation of nutrients, and body temperature maintenance. Without enough water, we won’t survive. We lose two to three liters of water daily—from sweating, urinating, defecating and even breathing—that needs to be replenished.

Water’s amazing benefits cannot be overstated. Inappropriately, some of us are substituting soda and other drinks, such as protein drinks for our water intake. Good news is that on average, our soda intake is down to 44 gallons of soda per year, while water is up to about 58 gallons. I stand guilty of not drinking enough water. I confess that drinking water has been a personal challenge, with tea being my drink of choice. And yet, when I don’t drink enough water, I experience dehydration and adverse symptoms, including fatigue, headaches and dry skin. Part of my morning ritual is setting an intention to drink water as a form of self-care.

It used to be that doctor’s recommended that we drink approximately eight glasses a day, however, new guidelines say we should drink anywhere from 2.0 to 3.7 liters (8.4 to 15.6 cups) daily, depending on our sex, weight, health, and environment. We might ask, what kind of water to drink with so many choices isuch as electrolyte-enhanced water, water with an alkaline pH level, collagen-infused water, distilled water, and water purified through reverse osmosis. Whatever your choice: The takeaway is to drink water as your primary beverage regularly and completely. Water is medicine!

"The most important part of the diet is
to eat with gratitude and love..."
Dr. U-Shaka Ra-Nebu Anpu

Love, a Macronutrient

As Tina Turner sings, "What's love got to do with it?" Everything. Love is an essential macronutrient, synthesizing all the other elements we consume into the 30 trillion cells within our bodies. It's one of the main ways the body processes energy; it rejuvenates our cells and heals wounds. Conversely, a lack of love is associated with poor health, stress, anxiety, emotional imbalance, antisocial behavior, chronic illness, heart disorders, unhappiness, and unhealthiness. Without love, our energy becomes blocked, the timing in our body is off and our life force becomes sluggish.

Slowly, research is beginning to show the importance of love in protecting us against health problems. For example, Dr. Richard Gerber writes in his book *Vibrational Medicine* that "children with asthma often come from families where the mother(father) is overprotective ... the child is smothering from an imbalanced expression of parental love, affecting the heart center." Have you ever felt true love? Have you noticed a difference in the choices you make in your life? How did you feel? Did you feel healthy?

Causes of love deficiency include early insecurities,

dysfunctional parenting, and various emotional factors. Through our personal life experiences, emotional deficiencies, and unstable inner and outer environments, the expression of love becomes distorted. For example, was your mother controlling or overprotective? Some caretakers are physically and mentally abusive; others are lenient and neglectful. Was your parent distant? When we don't love ourselves, we can't love others. Our love deficiency spills over into our food behavior such that the things we cook are filled with disappointments, regrets, and longings. Although they may be edible, they may not be nourishing or nurturing. Later in life, we may experience a failure to thrive due to years of love deficiency. Where does love come from? Love is innate energy that becomes awaken in our interactions with ourselves and others. As energy, love flows from the outside in and the inside out; from ourselves into our environments, our family and friends. Love as an ingredient in our food is a super nutrient.

Nourish yourself. Open your love or heart energy located near the center of the chest, behind the sternum. Tap into your love center. Feel compassion and engage in selfless service. Forgive ourselves and forgive others. Love heals the lungs, breast, and circulatory, respiratory, and immune systems. Love inspires, facilitates creativity, regulates mood and emotions, heal our bodies and minds, and transforms our lives. Above all, if you're cooking, do it with love, not begrudgingly; and if you're eating, do it lovingly.

Gunas (Nature)

Did you say what is this? Is it something to eat? No, *Gunas* may be one of the least familiar terms to us. Nonetheless, it's worth knowing it as we take this journey toward healthiness. Along with the macronutrients, minerals, vitamins, and love within our foods, there is energy or a life force. Through my yoga practice and Ayurvedic studies, I learned about gunas. Ayurveda reveals three gunas, or natures of ingredients: sattvic, rajasic, and tamasic. These primal natures are inherent in the foods we eat and affect how we feel. For example, sattvic foods, which are calming, include nuts, seeds, healthy oils, nonmeat proteins, and good carbohydrates, like fresh fruit, vegetables, legumes, and whole grains. Sattvic foods cultivate a peaceful mind.

While, Rajasic foods are stimulating and include onions, garlic, spiced or salty foods, sugar, chocolate, and caffeinated drinks, like soft drinks. These foods create an overly stimulating imbalance in the body, though occasionally, we might need a little stimulation. Finally, tamasic foods include alcohol, leftovers, meat, fish, mushrooms, overripe and underripe fruits, and vegetables. Generally, Tamasic foods sap our energy and weaken our minds tend to be heavily processed, sugary, and composed of refined carbohydrates, which de-energizes us and weakens our minds.

Of course, this information on the gunas is not meant to be comprehensive, but it is enough for us to realize that our food carries an energy, a nature, that can take us in one of two directions: toward health or toward disease. So, the next time you order one of those fancy-naming coffees, eat a meal in the restaurant, or grocery shop, read the nutrition facts labels on the back of the foods but also be mindful of the nature of the substances you're putting inside of your body. What we eat or drink may be tamasic or rajasic. Ask yourself, does this food make me feel calm, excited or tired? Are you already angry ingesting heated foods compounding your anger?

The key to understanding these forces of nature is realizing that they are all interrelated and continually changing. Meanwhile, our body intelligence is always seeking homeostasis, or equilibrium, between these interdependent elements to maintain our physiological, psychological and spiritual systems. Thus, knowing the inherent energetic force within our food encourages a way of life that is balancing and healing. Food is not merely a substance that we eat or drink to survive but a storehouse of universal energy and healthy vibrations that help us fulfill our purpose.

Insight: Change Our "What" and We Change Our Life

The bottom line is the "what" matters. So, just for moment, reflect on what you're putting in your mouth right now. Current research is showing that weight gain is due to more what we're eating than even how much. Considering that, become mindful of those fancy coffee drinks that gives us 6.5 to 10 percent of our recommended daily sodium, 20.4 percent of the maximum amount of saturated fat we are supposed to eat in a day, and a whopping 132 percent of the recommended daily allowance of sugar for women, or 91.6 percent for men? Stop over-treating yourself to the sweet and salty stuff. Everything we eat counts. *Wellness Begins Inside*

WHERE

Eating properly does not need to be complex. It simply entails eating the right food, in the right proportion, at the right time with the right attitude.
—Pandit Rajmani Tigunait, PhD

We eat everywhere. We eat at work, at home, in restaurants, in stores, and in our cars. We eat on our couches, in our beds, on the floor, in the street, in schools, on military bases, on airplanes, on trains, and even in prisons. We eat at fast food places, gas stations, bus stops, convenience stores, and in front of the television. We eat when walking down the street and when traveling in other countries. But does it matter where we eat?

We wouldn't eat in the bathroom, right? Or a restaurant that looked noticeably dirty? Why? Because it's disgusting. Where we eat affects our appetite, mood, and health. Have you ever sat down to eat and lost your appetite? Have you ever been to a noisy restaurant and eaten fast because you just wanted to leave? Perhaps, we've become so accustomed to noisy eating, fast food, and eating among strangers that it doesn't bother us.

Without a doubt, one of our favorite places to eat is ... out. Americans spend nearly fifty cents on food eaten outside the home for every dollar spent on food eaten at home. We consume at least one-third of our total calories eating out. That includes take-out food. The average American eats over four meals—that is, two meals and enough snacks to be calorically equivalent to an additional two meals—outside the home weekly, which means that on average, we're eating thirty percent of our total meals out. Regardless of what we're eating, we're eating out a lot. So, where's our favorite place to outsource our meals? More than half of the people who participated in a recent survey reported that 21.4 percent of their meals were prepared outside the home. Additionally, 90 percent of millennials—people born between 1981 and 1996, otherwise referred to as Generation Y—eat out compared to nearly three-fourths of the remaining population.

One of the reasons millennials give for their tendency to eat out is that they lack time to cook or even go to the grocery store. They also list their preference for a variety of foods as a reason for eating out. Meals outside the home make up 30 percent of evening meals, while another 34 percent are a mixture of home-cooked and prepared meals. So, nearly 65 percent of meals include prepared foods, while only about 35 percent are made entirely at home.

Although there is little research regarding whether where we eat matters, intuitively, it seems like it does. For example, some data suggests that if we're eating around people that consume a lot, we may mirror that behavior. So, our dining-out groups might contribute to our weight gain. Brian Wansink of Cornell University, author of *Mindless Eating: Why*

We Eat More Than We Think, says that where we eat may encourage us to eat more than we need. Often overlooked is the fact that when we're eating in the same space as others, we're also sharing their energy or vibration. If the energy is loud, chaotic, and fast, then the food carries that energy. I've been in restaurants where the conversations are loud, the food is hurried, and the plates contain at least three thousand calories, given the portion sizes. Amid the noise, you wonder as you look at your plate, *Am I supposed to eat all this food?* As such, it looks like outside environments are more conducive to eating more, not less.

Did you know that where we eat affects our digestive systems, moods, and even appetites? Eating around certain people can affect our appetite. At a conference, I found myself not wanting to eat with the groups because of the subtle, unwelcoming energy. It wasn't the food, but the people. Earlier, we talked about the gunas, or nature, of food. Well, just as there are sattvic, rajasic, and tamasic foods, our eating environments carry specific energies. Sattvic environments are uncluttered, peaceful, calming, and relaxing. Cell phones are turned off, as is the television, and we're mindful that we're eating. Bars are usually rajasic environments, with their multiple TVs blaring the sports news accompanied by the sounds of loud, intoxicated people. A tamasic setting is even more cluttered, unclean, and poorly maintained. Have you ever eaten in such an environment? I have and felt unnerved afterwards.

One day, I ordered a plant-based meal from this popular, pricey restaurant. Even before my meal arrived, a feeling came over me. I wanted to leave quickly. Only after I was outside did, I realized what it was: the environment was loud, overstimulating, and hurried. It was rajasic. After I walked out the door, away from the excessive noise, and into the fresh air, I noticed the difference. Have you ever been in an environment and felt drained? It is subtle but real. Suddenly you feel tired, inert, and even uninspired. Were the tables cluttered or too close together? Was the room dark? How did you feel? Everything possesses energy, a vibratory nature, including the environment where we eat. Is it quiet, clean? Are we eating in a peaceful environment? The places we choose to eat ought to be calm and relaxed, whether we're meat-eaters, vegetarians, or raw-food eaters.

Don't think that just because you're a plant-based eater it doesn't matter. Our eating environments leave an impression on our minds and our digestive systems. You could be eating a sattvic meal in a rajasic environment, which might nullify the food's possibly healthy nature. Food delivers the healing powers it embodies to promote balance. Environment matters. Why? Because the environment is also food.

I've eaten at my fair share of places, from high-end restaurants to fast-food establishments, from food carts on college campuses, at international restaurants, and in people's homes; I've eaten at low-end places, high-end places everything in between. I've eaten in dirty places and in clean places. At the time, socialization was more important than the environment. Gradually, however, I stop compromising my environments, and the most suitable place for me to eat became home. At that moment, I took an oath to serve myself and others the healthiest foods in a sattvic environment. So, whether we are outsourcing our meals or cooking them at home, the environment matters. The choice is up to us. Although family dinnertime is declining, here is the verdict: Home-cooked meals are better. The benefits include (1) healthier eating, (2) smaller portions, and (3) fewer carbohydrates, less sugar, and fat and better health.

WHEN

When walking walk. When eating eat.
—Buddha

When do you eat? Do you eat when you wake up in the morning or wait until midday? Are you a habitual snacker? Or do you eat when something bothers you? Do you eat when you're hungry? Does it make a difference? According to the science of chronobiology, the study of the natural physiological rhythms and other recurring phenomena; it does.

Our time and rhythm are off when it comes to eating. Unlike during the nineteenth century, when we ate for fuel and survival, nowadays, we may eat when we're not biologically hungry but bored or stressed. It's something to do. In this modern era, we're more situational eaters. Our eating is tied to situations like watching television and to heightened emotional periods, such as break-ups, job dissatisfaction and stress-related conditions. Our minds convince us we're hungry when we're not. When we do that, we often go against our natural biological clocks, which tell us that certain times are better to eat than others; daylight rather than nighttime.

What are those times? For one, studies indicate that late eating ramps up our bodies, 'which interferes with our circadian rhythms (circa about: diem: a day) or the 24 hours in the day/night cycle. Are you a late-night eater? Science informs us that our cortisol levels peak at around 7 a.m. to wake us up and drop to their lowest at 3 a.m. the next day before rising back to their peak five hours later. And so, morning is a favorable time to eat. Sunlight or an alarm can wake us up, and when that happens, the adrenal glands and the brain start to pump adrenalin. Meanwhile, the cortisol levels start dropping by mid-morning, while the adrenalin (for energy) and sorption (a mood stabilizer) keep pumping. At midday, our metabolisms and core body temperatures ramp up, priming us for hunger and eating. After that, cortisol levels start their decline. Metabolism slows down, and tiredness sets in. Gradually, serotonin turns into melatonin, which induces sleepiness. Our blood sugar levels decrease, and at 3 a.m., when we are in the middle of our sleep, cortisol levels hit their twenty-four-hour low. And so, our eating should not be random but regulated and mindful.

I come from a culture in which most meals were cooked at home following the tradition of eating breakfast, lunch, dinner, and occasional snacks. When I grew up, fast food did not exist, and frozen foods were only available to you if you could afford a freezer, so absolutely no meals were prepared outside the home. Food was controlled and regulated, with meals ending at specific times of the day, unlike twenty-four-hour dining of today. Rather than three meals, for nearly 2 decades, I've eaten one main meal daily, timing my meal for around noon, or midday. Earlier in my life, as a young adult, I abandoned the schedule of three daily meals that had marked my childhood. Instead, I ate when I chose, which was "whenever."

My former "whenever" eating schedule was not unusual; it's actually a norm today. I'm not alone. Still, our eating schedules as a nation have changed drastically between the Industrial Age and now. Studies show that America's typical three meals a day are a thing of the past, with nearly three-quarters of Americans no longer eating traditional breakfasts, lunches, and dinners. Research into the eating habits of two thousand Americans found that the traditional meal structure of breakfast, lunch, and dinner is followed by only 27 percent of people today. However, other sources indicate some Americans still eat three meals during the day: breakfast, lunch, and dinner. The specific timing for these meals varies by schedule and family, but we typically eat breakfast sometime between 7 am and 8 am, lunch between 12 pm and 2 pm, and dinnertime between 6 pm and 8 pm. Those three meals are usually supplemented by snacking throughout the day.

Snacking is linked to our personal cravings, with the average person eating five snack meals each week. On average, the people surveyed were most likely to eat two meals and three snacks in a typical day. However, research conducted by One Poll in conjunction with Farm Rich found that more and more Americans are opting for "snack meals" in place of three meals per day, with 86 percent of respondents revealing that they have replaced at least one traditional meal with a snack meal. Lunch, for 49 percent of Americans, is the meal most often replaced with snacks with the number one snack being chocolate. Whether at home or at work, respondents of all ages reported that their peak snacking hours were between 1 pm and 4 pm.

Noma Nazish, in the article *This Is the Best Time to Eat*

Breakfast, writes *that* the experts advise the best time to eat breakfast is within two hours of waking up. "The sooner you eat breakfast after you wake up, the better it is for your metabolism," says Kim Larson, Seattle-based dietitian, nutritionist and founder of Total Health. In addition, we should limit our meals and snacks to a ten-to-twelve-hour period during the day and avoid eating later in the evening. For example, only eat between 6 a.m. and 6 p.m. or between 7 a.m. and 5 p.m.

Do you go to the gym in the morning? Then it's advisable morning to consume a light meal, like a banana or avocado toast, twenty to thirty minutes before your workout. When it comes to dinner, the average time at which people eat is 6:22 pm. Of course, it varies considerably and can be anywhere between 4:30 pm and 10:59 pm. Dinner, ranks as the main meal in the United States.

Clearly, Americans have shifted away from the traditional meal structure from 180 years ago, and no longer is our eating dependent on the sun or weather. Instead, we eat whenever we want—allocating about 32,098 hours in our lifetimes to eating and drinking. According to the Bureau of Labor Statistics, we spend approximately 1 hour and 8 minutes consuming food and drink every weekday with not much more than that on weekends and holidays—only around 1 hour and 17 minutes.

So, if we're not spending a lot of time out of twenty-four hours of a day eating, how is it that more than 30 percent of adults aged twenty and over are obese (including 7.6 percent with severe obesity) and another 31.8 percent overweight? In the last thirty years, obesity rates have doubled in adults, tripled in children, and quadrupled in adolescents. Moreover, our unhealthy diets contribute to approximately 678,000 deaths each year in the US due to nutrition and obesity-related diseases, such as heart disease, cancer, and type 2 diabetes. Thus, while the amount of time we spend eating is modest, we're jeopardizing our health with both our food choices, sedentary lifestyle, and when we eat.

A recent study revealed that weight loss, a much talked about aspiration for most people, has given rise to an over one-billion-dollar industry. Losing weight, however, may come down also to *when* we're eating along with what we eat. According to the survey, if losing weight is your focus, you should eat your last meal of the day by 2 p.m. In addition, researchers at the University of Alabama Birmingham looked into early time-restricted feeding (eTRF)—an approach in which your dinnertime moves to the afternoon instead of the evening. According to *The Diet Review*, a publication of Harvard Medical School, a moderate level of research suggests that eTRF may have some benefit in terms of reducing the risk of chronic diseases.

According to Dr. Edward Bitok, who is an assistant professor in the Department of Nutrition and Dietetics of the Loma Linda University School of Allied Health Professions, the wait time between meals should be between *three* and *five* hours. This waiting period is ideal, he explained, because it is the average time it takes to empty the stomach's contents into the small intestine after a standard meal.

Analogous to a budget, we don't know how much we are spending or what we're buying until we write it down. Sometimes, we don't know when or what we're eating until we journal it. Do you eat five meals a day, including two snacks? Have you ever thought about how often you eat? Whatever we put in our mouths counts as a food or food-like substance, so you could be eating three meals daily with five snacks, which gives you a total of eight meals daily. Perhaps you eat one meal a day with snacks.

If we eat three nutrient-dense meals a day and two healthy

snacks, consuming between 1800-2000 calories daily, our bodies should be more than adequately fueled. And when synchronized with our circadian rhythms—our twenty-four-hour internal clocks—our meals provide us with at least twelve hours of optimum energy. Nutrient-dense diets include at least five servings of fruits and vegetables.

Insight:

The optimal food intake interval for good health, including physical harmony and metabolic balance, is every two to three 2-3 hours. Nutritionists point out that eating small, frequent meals helps maintain metabolic integrity. When should we stop eating? Our last meal should be three hours before we go to bed, preferably around 6:00 pm. As a rule of thumb, we shouldn't eat right before bed because it increases our blood sugar and insulin and affects our ability to sleep.

When we eat affects our metabolism, body weight, blood sugar, insulin, digestive system, and sleep cycle. Snacking is not essential, but a choice. When we eat our meals and snack, it should not be random but calibrated with our bodies' natural food processing rhythm. Unfortunately, most of us eat whenever we feel like it. It doesn't matter to us, yet it does matter to our bodies regarding weight and our overall health. If we adhere to the body's natural rhythm, we will find that there is a time to digest and a time to rest; there is a time for hunger and a time for sleep. Changing our "whenever" eating philosophy to mindful timing supports a healthy body.

WAY

People who eat slowly are less likely to become obese or develop metabolic syndrome, a cluster of heart disease, diabetes, and stroke risk factors.
—The American Heart Association

Have you ever sat across a person eating with their mouths open? Every time they chew, you can see food just churning around. Or what about someone who hold their utensils like a weapon shoving food in their mouths or someone who keep their elbows on the table? Do you text while eating or keep your cell phone nearby? Are you one of those people who pick up your plate or bowl and bring it to your mouth? Do you pick over your food, frowning instead of smiling? These are a few examples of the ways we eat, and of course, there are others. For instance, we used to sit at the table at dinnertime; now, we sit on the couch, floor, or wherever. A recent study revealed that 48 percent of people don't eat dinner at an actual table. Aside from cultural differences, in the United States the way we eat is less communal, focused or ritualistic.

Since the Colonial period (1492–1763) and the Industrial Age, our eating behaviors have changed. In the eighteenth century, influenced by Europe, our table manners consisted of eating at a table, sitting down, and using utensils, like forks and even knives. Prior to that "'Eating had often been a causal, ad hoc and untidy nonevent that made little use of tables and chairs, required no utensils, and bore few if any social expectations'" writes Abigail Carroll in Three Squares, The Invention of the American Meal, 2013, pp. 6–6. Fast forward to today. We're back to an impromptu style which includes walking and eating, eating while standing, and often eating with our fingers. It wasn't always that way. John Daly writes in the article *What is etiquette, and where did it originate?* The first known etiquette book was written in 2400 B.C. by an African sage, Ptahhotep which lets us know manners have been around for a while. At present though, our social decorum has given way to a more relaxed and carefree eating attitude and social interaction. Time and cultural shifts have swung the pendulum back, to eating as if we were living in a colonial period of time

Our way of eating is individualized, but also class oriented. That is, we eat the way, we've learned; and what our environment tolerates. Holding our utensils, a certain way, and our approach to eating is all learned. Have you ever seen someone grab the handle of their fork, and shove the food on it? Watch a toddler just learning to use utensils, and you might see some resemblance? The *way* means a "method, style, or manner of doing something" such as eating. Etiquette is taught either directly or indirectly. If you're not taught to hold your fork with the teeth pointing downwards with your index finger on the handle, then you'll grab it and hold it like a pitchfork.

In addition to the historical influences on the ways we eat, we are also impacted by the different standards each home maintains—that is, we are subject to the norms within our households. And yet, despite the differences in our historical or household ways, we commonly employ the same tools and body parts to put food in our mouth. For example, we use our eyes, mouths, teeth, throats, esophagus, and digestive systems to eat. Culturally, some of us eat with our hands, use bread as a utensil or with chopsticks, others with forks, spoons, and knives. Regardless of the tools, eating consists of using apparatuses or utensils in collaboration with the body and food. So, the way we eat involves history, culture, and specific environment and biological attributes, but I've also discovered what I refer to as another way which taps into our "mental memories" surrounding food and eating. These mental memories inform the way we eat.

Let me share with you two of my earlier mental memories of eating. The first is of sitting on a bench facing a bowl of pokeweed in a large room with many other children. At the time, we were called "throwaways." The atmosphere was one of survival, where you ate fast, and literary stuff food in your mouth with your hands for fear of the food disappearing. So, it wasn't unusual to see children guarding by curving their arms around the rim of their food plates with one hand and using the other to dive into their food. This environment shaped the way I ate later on until I was scolded to not eat that way. The second memory comes from a different environment. I was sitting at a medium-sized kitchen table with two siblings and silently swinging my legs. There we used the typical eating tools—spoon and fork—and no longer guarded our food. However, before touching my food, I was reminded to say grace: "Bless us, oh Lord, and these thy gifts which we are about to receive from thy bounty through Christ our

Lord, Amen." Since grace was requisite before eating, I said it. Under the glare of an unhappy caretaker, I poked around my food, rarely eating all of it. Table manners were strictly enforced, because one's manners indicated one's class. For starters, no elbows were allowed on the table, and there was no smacking of your mouth. Farting at the table was an offense, but an even graver was laughing at the offensive behavior. Two different environments, but eating remain a survival process, not one based on enjoyment.

In the household, I grew up being civilized and mannerly was a reflection of the person raising you. At that time, it was an unspoken message that Negroes ate like animals. And even though you couldn't change your race, you could change the way you ate. The last thing you wanted to do is bring shame on your family because of the lack of proper table manners. Being a colored girl, a heavy emphasis was placed on not acting like a "pickaninny," a disparaging term used to refer to a young, black, ill-bred child. One way of displaying the fineness of American cultural norms at the time was the way in which we ate all of our meals. Although we couldn't afford to adhere to all of the mores of the early nineteenth century, which included eating salad and desserts at dinner, the way we interacted with food at the table was of utmost concern, not so much the content of the food. It was so important that my eating habits was closely monitored.

Of course, choosing a favorite meal was not an option. You ate what was placed before you. Holidays were slightly different only because the menu changed; the atmosphere stayed the same. Maybe this heaviness in the air had to do with the hands that prepared the meal, which was a relic of the Great Depression survivor. Her survival experiences permeated the meals. Stark reminders of food scarcity were evident in her red OPA ration tokens, which she treasured. These rations represented a history that fed her stern and serious attitudes surrounding food. She demanded that nothing be left on the plate or thrown away. Her experiences molded the way I ate, with food taking on a different meaning for me. Although no joy came from my experience of sitting in the small, rectangular kitchen, facing this foe on my plate was complicated. Nonetheless, I've learned that the mental memories we bring to the plate speak volumes about the ways we eat.

I shared with you two environments that influenced my eating, which speaks to my feelings or memories. Having been in many different places, I always felt that deep down, the way I ate was informed by a mixture of scarcity, rigidity, and indifference. With certainty, I say that within my restricted atmosphere, my stomach would tighten and cramp up when it came to mealtimes. This caused me to be one of those picky eaters, often preferring to get it over with and leave the table.

Think about your way of eating. Do you eat quickly? Fast eating is pretty standard nowadays, even though some of us still eat slowly. Studies show that people in America eat too fast, sometimes in about two minutes, while multitasking. This speed eating is coupled with mindlessness. We eat to get it out of the way so we can move on to other activities. Perhaps, we have forgotten the food scarcity of the Great Depression and therefore take food for granted in this modern era with so many food choices and fast-food eateries. Unfortunately, though, our fast-eating style comes with some health challenges. For example, fast eating stimulates weight gain and increases the number of calories we consume.

When we eat too fast, we bypass the signal that tells us we're full. As a result, we eat more than we should and rarely feel this sense of fullness. Also, eating fast causes more significant glucose fluctuations, leading to a breakdown in the way our muscle, fat, and liver cells respond to insulin.

When that happens, our bodies don't receive glucose from our blood, and extra stress is placed on our pancreases to produce more insulin to provide glucose for our cells. This condition is known as insulin resistance. In contrast, slower eating results in us eating fewer calories, because we feel fuller sooner.

Of course, the way we eat is not only about the pace but also our mental attitudes and eating practices. Earlier, I shared my mental memories. One practice that stands out for me is praying over or blessing our food. Is saying grace before we eat a lost practice? When is the last time you witnessed someone praying before they ate? How many of us pray before we eat? Of course, various reasons exist why people pray or don't pray before meals, from political affiliations to religious views to a lack of exposure to the practice. According to a new survey by the *Washington Post* and the Kaiser Family Foundation, about half of all Americans say a prayer over their food at least a few times a week. The other half dig right into the food, unaware or resistant to the need to offer gratitude. When we do that, we treat food as a given, not a gift.

Throughout my life, I've forgotten to offer gratitude over my food or resisted doing so depending on who I was around, but as I've progressed on my spiritual journey, I've remembered the scarcity of food, the hands of the Great Depression survivor, and the hundreds of people dying from starvation. I'm grateful and thankful for the plant, vegetable and mineral kingdom that make it possible for me to exist. Now, I unapologetically express my gratitude for the food I eat with prayer.

Of course, the ways we eat are varied. But ask yourself, is your chosen way of eating improving your health or damaging it? Not only research but also my direct experience suggests that the way of eating matters. As I reflect on my eating experiences, I recognize that unlearning is part of my journey. I learned that the ways we eat reflect our prior eating experiences. Eating fast, eating with our mouths open, eating on the go, and eating with negative attitudes affect our eating experiences. Even though we're adults, some of eat like toddlers with all of the emotional messaging that accompanies it.

As I sought to change the way I ate, I return to my food story. Once I figure out the answers to a few questions, my eating practices changed. Two of the fundamental ways I've changed is to view eating as a ritual. Another way has been to enjoy food and let go of my past negative experiences surrounding it. Our ways of eating are worth exploring, because they could mean the difference between health or illness, enjoyment or duty. I believe our bodies digest not only food but the mindset that accompanies it. Take a moment to reflect on the way you eat. Write down five words to describe your eating style.

I began asking myself questions like, *Why am I rushing through my meal? No one is going to take it away from me*, and *Why did I not say grace? Am I taking this food for granted?* We read so much about what not to eat that we have forgotten the way we eat empowers us with energy, with life force. Children coming from food-impoverished atmospheres like I did respond differently than those who come from environments where food is abundant. By understanding our past experiences, we transition from unconscious to conscious eating. We become present with our food and change the way we approach our meals.

Insight:

According to experts, we should allocate at least thirty minutes for our meals. Bring a positive attitude to the plate.

Adopt an attitude of mindfulness, or conscious eating. Let's change the way we eat by becoming aware that we're chewing, swallowing, and even digesting. Retrain yourself to hold your utensil properly, to appreciate the experience of eating. Be present. Allow your taste buds the chance to enjoy your food by slowing down. Relax your mind and release the memories that block your ability to receive the complete nutrients of the food. Finally, take a few moments before eating to express gratitude for the minerals, the plant and vegetable kingdom, and if you eat meat, the animal kingdom. Make eating a sacred ritual.

Don't take another mouthful before you have
swallowed what is in your mouth.
—Malagasy Proverb

THE SINISTER S'S

One who loves you, warns you.
-African Proverb

Sugar

Nina Simone sings, "I want a little sugar in my bowl. I want a little sweetness down in my soul." Who doesn't like sweets, desserts? Whether it's ice cream, candy bars, water ice, cakes, pies, cookies, sodas, sweet drinks, snack bars, cereal, or something else, that sweetness lives within our cells, not our souls. Rarely do we refuse the sweet stuff. The moment that sweet taste touches our tongues, we feel a rush and want more. Some call it a "sugar high." If it sounds like an addiction, that's because it is. According to several sources, sugar releases dopamine and serotonin, hormones in the brain known to make us feel good and happy. Alexis Conason, Psy.D. in Sugar addiction | Psychology Today shares that research conducted by Dr. Eric Stice, a neuroscientist at the Oregon Research Institute reveals that sugar activates the same brain regions that are activated when a person consumes drugs like cocaine.

Our sugar cravings tap into the same areas of the brain associated with drug addiction. Few of us would consider ourselves addicts, because we don't define sugar as a drug, but with the way we consume sugar, we each need to stand up and say, "Greetings, my name is ... and I'm an addict." We need to go to sugar rehab. I wanted to learn more about this growing silent addiction causing serious damage in our lives.

Here's proof of our sugar jonesing: Around the early nineteenth century, we ate only 2 pounds of sugar annually on average. Around 1970 or 150 years later, we were up to eating 123 pounds of sugar per year. That's a 6,050 percent increase in our sugar intake. We currently consume almost 152 pounds of sugar in one year, which equates to 3 pounds of sugar consumed weekly, with our children ingesting a whopping 19 teaspoons of added sugar daily. Between 1970 and today, our sugar habit has grown 24 percent. Go to the supermarket and look at your food's content; more than fifty percent of products contain added sugar. It's evident as a society, we're trending in an unhealthy direction regarding this sweet stuff.

If someone were to ask us what these small, innocent-looking white cubes on the tables or the seemingly healthy brown crystal versions in packets we use on and in our food were, our response would be, sugar. But what is sugar? Sugar is a dissolvable carbohydrate, a macronutrient, and an energy source—all elements that we need for life. It goes by various aliases: sugar, glucose, honey, sorghum syrup, lactose, fruit juice concentrate, high-fructose corn syrup (HFCS), dextrose, agave, fructose, caster sugar, corn syrup, sorbitol, molasses, maltose, corn sweetener, sucrose (table sugar), brown sugar, and syrup. Most of all, these tiny crystals carry a lot of sway in our lives.

This raises the question how can we need something and not need it at the same time? Well, I found out that all sugar is not equal, yet as the saying goes, "A rose by any other name would smell as sweet." The names of sugar do not affect its actual nature. Where the difference lies is in the types of sugar we consume—that is, whether they are complex and natural or simple and processed. It takes our bodies longer to break down the long molecular chains of glucose or natural sugar. This longer digestion time gives us more continuous energy and helps us avoid blood sugar and insulin spikes. It also promotes feelings of fullness and prevents overeating.

Conversely, processed sugar, bum-rushes our systems and is absorbed quickly, with the small intestine's enzymes breaking it down into glucose. This fast ingestion is problematic because it overrides the leptin hormone which interferes with the body's natural ability to detect fullness. Simply stated, with processed sugars, we overeat and our bodies save the extra calories as fat, which causes health problems, such as obesity. Natural sugars come from whole, natural foods, including fruit and vegetables, such as carrots, beets, squash, zucchini, and onions. Examples of processed or refined sugar include white cane sugar, high-fructose corn syrup, and the currently popular sweetener, agave.

Whether eating a mango, a slice of cake or drinking a soda, we need to become mindful of our body's response when we indulge in excessive sugar. When we eat, the stomach digests our food. This food, known as carbohydrates (sugars and starches), breaks down into another sugar type, called glucose (blood sugar), which is absorbed into our bloodstream. When this happens, the glucose does one of two things: immediately converts to energy or is stockpiled in our bodies for later use. Insulin, a hormone made and monitored by the beta cells in the pancreas, helps this glucose travel into our body to be used for energy or storage. Without insulin, our blood sugar stays high, which is a problem. For example, when we eat high- carbohydrates foods, like white bread, white rice, and pasta, we raise the glucose levels in our blood, triggering the pancreas to release more insulin into the bloodstream to control it. Without insulin, blood sugar levels stay high, creating a disaster.

Our challenge in eating is in consuming the right amount of glucose for energy and balancing it with just the right amount of insulin. Only then can our bodies maintain the energy needed for life and our daily activities. Balance is the key. Unfortunately, if our body stops producing any or enough insulin, or if our cells become resistant to it, we can suffer from diabetes, triggering our blood sugar levels to rise to dangerous levels. In the article "16 Subtle Symptoms You're Eating Too Much Sugar" by Colleen de Bellefonds, she writes that Karen Ansel, RD, an author of Healing Superfoods for Anti-Aging, says we're finding out more all the time about the adverse health effects of too much insulin in our bloodstreams."

When we consume too much sugar, we are at risk for obesity, type 2 diabetes, and heart disease. Likewise, excess sugar increases susceptibility to cell damage, cancer, chronic disease, inflammation, chronic disease, liver disease, and tooth decay. Thus, that sweet stuff that we crave so much also makes us prone to depression and dementia.

The good news is that today, we scan any nutrition facts label labels and see that sugar is a popular additive in our foods. And so, we can regulate what goes inside our bodies. According to the Academy of Nutrition and Dietetics, of the more than 85,000 food products sold in the United States, 74% contain added sugars. Look on any label, and you'll undoubtedly find sugar and added sugar, even if the product doesn't taste sweet. That's true of bread, such as tomatoes, sauces, in general, and protein bars, sugary drinks, candy, baked goods, and sweetened dairy products.

Sugar, aka diabetes, was the cause of death for most of my family members. A challenge is that added sugars can be hard to spot on nutrition facts labels since they can be listed under several aliases, such as corn syrup, agave nectar, palm sugar, cane juice, and sucrose. No matter the name, it's all glucose to the body, and an excess of it damages the body.

Think about this, we're consuming 42.5 teaspoons of sugar a day, which means that six hundred eighty (33–34 percent) of our daily calories are coming from our sugar habits. Wherein we should actually only be obtaining 10 percent of our calories from sugar, which equals 13.3 teaspoons of sugar per day (based on a 2,000-calorie-per-day diet). Did you know that eating an orange contributes less sugar to the body than drinking orange juice? That's because the fiber helps regulate the amount of fructose the body absorbs and because a serving of orange juice contains the equivalent of four oranges. That means that orange juice contains about 24 grams (6 teaspoons) of sugar per 8 ounce serving. In fact, orange juice and orange soda have similar sugar contents, and both can have unhealthy effects, such as causing weight gain. Sure, the words *orange* and *apple* or the names of any fruit sound nutritional before your drink, but what does that mean? I know we all like our juices, but even drinking more than 5 ounces (150 milliliters) per day is unhealthy. By now, we know that too much sugar harms the body, but we don't know, or maybe are reluctant to admit, that we're powerless to stop without support, just as with any addiction. Similar to drugs, overeating, smoking, support is needed to cut back on our sugar dependency.

I am writing this book because of the indifference I witness among family and friends surrounding food choices contributing to their dis-ease. Too often, we're reluctant to share what is going on when we feel sick. We carry secrets and struggles within us concerning our heath, however ignoring our health is not the answer. Don't be ashamed of your health challenges; transform them. With my brother's hospitalization for a nephrectomy, the surgical removal of his kidney-I was there. That's right, we can live with one kidney, but if we can sustain them, why not? Shortly afterwards, about one year later, he was in the surgery suite for the removal of his second kidneys. With no kidneys and only this dialysis machine, other parts of his body rapidly degenerated. My first-time walking into a dialysis center, I cried. Just like that, my brother joined what he called the "club". He was not alone at the club. I felt powerless and frightened. Although he had been born with healthy kidneys, my brother's organs had deteriorated over the years. I knew that he ate some of the unhealthiest foods, mostly simple carbohydrates, and ultra-processed fast food and drank alcohol as his drink with reckless abandonment. Don't get me wrong, my brother was a hard-working, responsible, dedicated US government employee and the nicest person you will meet. But like far too many of us, he did not practice self-care. Health was non-issue.

Years before his kidney disease surfaced, I'd already embarked on my health journey. Going through his illness with him made me think we should all consider ourselves prediabetic, even if it doesn't yet show up in annual blood tests. It is showing up in our collective sugar consumption, so why wait? We shouldn't presume health but influence it. That's why, for years, I've checked my glucose. I also became mindful of my AC1 levels, which measure the percentage of hemoglobin proteins in our blood coated with sugar, or our average blood sugar levels over 60-90 days. The higher our A1C levels are, the greater our risk for developing type 2 diabetes, such as 5.7% to 6.4%. Do you know your A1C levels? So far, my fasting glucose has been good, but as I've gotten older, a slight increase in my AC1 levels has caused me to adjust my food intake accordingly.

Insight: Armed with knowledge of my family history of diabetes, I'm determined to listen to my body's needs and not my emotions. When we listen to our emotions, we do that crazy eating. I monitor, minimize, and eliminate the added and hidden sugar in foods and drinks with all that I've learned. When is the last time you had your AC1 levels checked? In memory of my brother, I'm committed to eradicating diabetes from my bloodline. Of course, we can only change ourselves. However, in doing so, we may just change other.

Sodium

Don't pass the salt, please. Did you notice that most restaurants no longer have saltshaker on the table? Of course, this is not a health decision, but supposedly one of table space. Do you have a saltshaker on your home table? Salt is one way we judge whether food is tasty. If there is little or no salt, we call it bland. These small, seemingly innocent granules are so powerful and plays a significant role in our lives. Although these little crystals are essential, they too complicate our lives when taken in excess. Going under many names, such as sodium chloride, sodium, and salt which is 40% sodium and 60% chloride, this macrominerals deserves special attention because it is associated with high blood pressure and both cardiovascular and kidney disease if used excessively. According to MacGregor and de Wardener, the use of added salt is a modern habit because our ancestors did not do it. To our harm, our food has become saltier over the years. Today, we're consuming salt at a rate ten to twenty times greater than we did five thousand years ago.

Like a conditioned reflex, sometimes, we don't realize we're adding salt to food that's already salted during processing or cooking. In fact, the salt added during processing accounts for about 80 percent of our salt intake. Of course, we need sodium, but too much over time contributes to high blood pressure and increases our risk of having a heart attack or stroke. As with sugar, we've acquired a taste for sodium at a level that puts us at risk for health problems. As a hypertensive society, with nearly half of American adults experiencing high blood pressure, we ignore one of the offenders. African-Americans have the highest prevalence of high blood pressure in the world. Some research even points to likelihood that African-Americans may be salt-sensitive and should be mindful of their sodium intake.

Insight: Few if any of us measure our salt intake. All of us could benefit in reducing our sodium use to 2,300 mg, or one teaspoon of salt, per day which include the sodium added during manufacturing or cooking especially if we're over fifty. Hypertension, however, is not a disease of an older population. High blood pressure in children and adolescents is not uncommon. A recent study that looked at fifteen thousand adolescents found that nearly one in five had hypertension. Whether older or younger, individuals diagnosed with high blood pressure or prehypertension should limit sodium intake to 1,500 milligrams per day, or about ⅔ teaspoon of salt.

Saturated Fats

Like most people, I never paid much attention to the fat content of my foods. All that changed when I began cooking and studying the effects that specific kinds of fat have on my health. Of course, if we eat out a lot, we rarely think about fat content. And, if we purchase cooking oils with words like *vegetable*, *palm*, *coconut*, and *nondairy alternative* in their names, we use them because they sound healthy. Besides, what's wrong with coconut and vegetables? Something sounding healthy doesn't mean it is. What we don't know can be harmful. Take saturated fats; these molecules full of hydrogen are unhealthy and detrimental.

If we care about our heart health, we become mindful of the effects of saturated fats. Did you know that sixty-three percent of the fat in butter is saturated fat? And palm oil contains about the same amount of saturated fats as butter? 6 g saturated fat. Coconut oil is 92% saturated fat and therefore raises cholesterol levels similar to animal fats (butter, lard). Or that a popular veggie burger includes 6 g saturated fat, which is considered high. Saturated fats are common and are found everywhere in our diet. What we ignore about our food infrastructure has devastating consequences on our lives.

So why is saturated fat unhealthy? Because it hardens at room temperature. Admittedly, that didn't mean too much to me initially, until I started digging deeper. By being solid, saturated fat is guilty of being a ringleader in heart disease and in increasing our harmful LDL cholesterol levels—the kind of cholesterol that blocks our arteries throughout the body. Cholesterol builds up in our blood vessels and increases our risks of heart disease and stroke.

What do we do? We should replace the foods in our diets high in saturated fats with those high in monounsaturated and polyunsaturated fats, which are generally found in plants and lauded as healthy fats. It also means eating fish and nuts and replacing meat with beans or legumes, seeds, avocados, whole grains, and vegetables. The main sources of saturated fat are mostly animal products, including red meat, whole milk, cheese, and other whole-milk dairy foods. Saturated fat can also be found in coconut, palm oil, and many commercially prepared baked goods and other foods. Meat is hands-down the biggest culprit in our high saturated fat consumption. Yet, with so many plant-based meat alternatives available, vegetarians fall into to trap of thinking that if it's not meat, then it's alright. But a lot of nonmeat products are high in saturated fats.

Our saturated fat intake is increasing. So far, it's gone from 11.5 to 11.9 percent of our daily calories. Data published in the *Journal of the American Medical Association* lets us know that our saturated fat intake has increased over the last eighteen years. And so, saturated fat consumption remains well above what it should be, which is *10 percent* of our daily calories. Our everyday indulgence comes packaged as red and processed meat, ultra-processed fast food, and low-quality carbohydrates, including sugary beverages, snacks, and refined grains.

According to the American Heart Association, our dietary regimens should allow for only 5 percent to 7 percent of our calories to come from saturated fat. Thus, we should limit saturated fat in our daily diets. If you're consuming 2,000 calories per day, then 7 percent of your calories would be 140. Divide that by 9, because there are 9 calories per gram of fat, and we get 15 grams of saturated fat.

Why is this important? Heart disease is the leading cause of death for men and women, and our children are inheriting our heart-unhealthy ways of living. It's time to reset, reverse, and change the course of our lives. Become mindful, selective, and discerning about the amount of saturated fat that enters your body. Read the nutrition fact labels. Replace foods high in saturated fat to save your life and those of your loved ones. Also, become mindful of your portions, or serving sizes. Don't exceed your saturated fat quota. Refrain from taking in more saturated fat than you can afford. Don't go into fat debt.

Insight: As I mentioned, this book is personal for me. I've witnessed too many unnecessary deaths based on ignorance, stubbornness, indifference and addiction to unhealthy lifestyles. Seldom do we make health a priority even during family gathering. Unfortunately, to many of us health is a non-issue. At one point, in the early morning, it wasn't unusual for me to receive calls that one of my brothers died from a heart attack. We ignore the foods contributing to our high cholesterol levels, damaged arteries, and deteriorating minds and bodies. One of my brothers survived on a daily intake of fast fried foods and 16 different pills for the following diseases: dangerously high cholesterol, which was over 300, diabetes, dangerously high blood sugar levels of over 300 mg/dL, clogged arteries, cardiovascular disorder and habitual insomnia. That's a lot of medicine. After heart surgery, he was released from the hospital to recover, and died from a heart attack.

Stress

We all know the feeling of stress, right? No one is given a waiver from stress. It's a feeling of tension and tightness, accompanied by a foreboding fear. These feelings affect our abilities to think and carry out our daily activities in life. The reasons we have these feelings vary from person to person, such as economics, relationships, health, school, employment, trauma, and lifestyle. Although stress has been around for eons, our modern-day stressors and stress responses are magnified by technology, social media, and the political climate. After a while, we neglect our bodies, minds, and spirits. Surely, our current pandemic has added stress to an already stressed society. With COVID-19 and the recent social unrest, our livelihoods have been threatened. Emotionally, we're feeling uncertain. With unemployment, educational shutdowns, quarantines, deaths, and overall uncertainty, we've gained weight and neglected to take care of ourselves. That weight is no joke. While some say we should focus on mental health, others say physical health. It can't be either-or; we must take a holistic approach to taking care of our minds, bodies, and spirits. At no other time in history has it been more critical that we have relaxation practices.

Many of us are suffering from compound stress—that is, we're already stressed, and yet we're adding on more stress, which becomes life threatening and exposes us to other health problems, like stomach ulcers, increased heart rate, high blood pressure, headaches, diabetes, hair loss, digestive/gastrointestinal problems, depression, anxiety, and, yes, weight gain and obesity. When stressed, we don't think clearly and feel overwhelmed. Our diets become rich in sugar, salt, and saturated fat. Many people reach for alcohol, drugs, or other vices. One woman I met had piercings all over her face, and tattoos that covered most of skin, I was curious and asked her why? She responded, "Every time I get stress this is what I get another piercing." Our stress-response is alive

Stress is a naturally occurring phenomenon. At one time or another, we all experience stress—some people more than others. For health reasons, we need to alleviate or reduce the chronic tension we carry around before our physical and mental health deteriorates. Chronic stress compromises our health. It's better to be proactive than reactive. The antidote to stress is to relax. I know this is easier said than done, but when I say "relax," I'm referring to bringing about a biological change in our bodies having to do with our autonomic nervous systems, which govern the sympathetic fight-or-flight response or the parasympathetic rest-and-digest response-to really relax. We can't fool the body and pretend to relax; it has to be real.

Relaxation involves the parasympathetic system. When we activate our parasympathetic systems, our blood pressure, heart rates, and breathing rates slow down, and the digestive system is regulated. Thus, to counter stress, a conscious, consistent effort and commitment must be made to activate our parasympathetic nervous systems with activities such as walking in nature, meditating, 61-Point relaxation meditation, vagus nerve practices, breathing deeply from the diaphragm, progressive and even practicing qigong and yoga. These activities enhance vagal toning and lower our cortisol levels so that we can *Wellness Begins Inside*.

Relaxation requires the support of the vagus nerve, the tenth cranial nerve in the parasympathetic nervous system. As our vagus nerve travels from the hypothalamus into the chest, diaphragm, and intestines, we connect with essential body functions controlling our emotions, moods, throat muscles, blood pressure, and digestion. With the vagus nerve two-way communicating system between the brain and organs—the heart, the lungs, and the gut—we breathe and eat better, control our weight, normalize our heart rates, stress less, and relax more.

Insight:

As we can see, something is always happening in our bodies because something is always happening outside our bodies. Whether its bills, health, relationships, work, or generalized fear and worry, stress is present. Whatever, stressors we are experiencing gets interpreted by the soul, body and mind. But we're not helpless or powerless, we get to choose how we interpret and respond to the uncertainties in life. With a practice, we learn to breathe, relax, and meditate to bring clarity to life's uncertainties.

Stress-Less

- Turn off the television, and pick up a book and read.
- Reduce your time on social media.
- Put your cell phone on silent or vibrate.
- Be discerning about who you follow and what you allow into your sensory system.
- Connect with positive energy.
- Be creative. Draw, paint, write, or even garden inside or outdoors.
- Sleep at least seven to eight hours.
- Activate your vagus nerves; engage in neck stretches.
- Connect with a yoga practice specifically designed to activate your rest-and-digest system and vagal toning.
- Learn relaxation breathing techniques.
- Increase your intake of vegetables and fruit.
- Listen to positive messages in music, lectures, and posts.
- Remember to laugh. Soften your face.
- Thoughts determine our reality. Transform your thoughts from stressing to relaxing.

"Don't get caught in the past, because the past is gone
Don't get upset about the future,
because the future is not yet here.
There is only one moment, for you to be
alive, and that is the present moment. Go
back to the present moment, and live this
moment deeply, and you'll be free.
***Knowing the Better Way To Live Alone*-Buddha**

NUTRITION FACT LABELS

Few of us keep track of how much sugar, saturated fat, and sodium we consume. Twenty-eight years ago, we couldn't because we didn't have access to that information. Nowadays, we do have access to some of the ingredient in our food because of nutritional labeling.

But it wasn't always that way. Before 1994, this information was unavailable to the consumer.

Twenty years later, in 2014, the FDA required nutrition facts labels to include the amount added sugar.

Daily value for 2000 calories diet daily

- **Serving Size**
- Calories in the serving size
- **Nutrient**
- Saturated fats
- Cholesterol
- Sodium
- **Total** Carbohydrates
- Dietary Fiber
- **Total Sugar**
- Added Sugar
- **Protein**
- **Vitamins**

Along with the sodium, saturated fat, and sugar contents, we also have serving sizes. Did you know that the factors determining the serving sizes listed on packaged foods and beverages are somewhat nebulous? Serving sizes are determined by how much of that item people *typically* consume at one time, rather than how much people *should* consume. And so, the responsibility falls on us to consider our bodies' needs as we examine the nutritional content, serving sizes and the timing of when we eat.

What We Should Be Consuming

Sugar	25 g (women)/36 g (men)	6–9 tsp.
Sodium	1,500–2,300 mg	⅔ to 1 tsp.
Saturated fat	22 g or less	5 ½ tsp.

Review
1. **If a label says that there are 12 grams of added sugar in a serving size of ½ cup, how much can you consume?**
2. **If a label says that the food contains 5.5 grams of saturated fat per serving, what should your daily intake be?**
3. **If a label says that there are 1,150 mg of sodium per serving, how many teaspoons are there? Is that more than the American Heart Association recommends consuming?**
Answer: 1) women= 1cup; 1 ½ cup for men daily. 2) 4 serving 3) ½ teaspoons. Less.

SUGGESTIONS FOR MEALS

Breakfast

Caloric content: 300–400 calories, or 30–35 percent of your daily food intake

The first meal of the day consists of us breaking our night-long fasts from eating. When you eat breakfast, consider when, why, what, and how you eat.

When

You should eat breakfast one to two hours after waking up. So if you wake up at 6 a.m., you should eat breakfast at 7 or 8 a.m.

Why

You're replenishing your glucose supply after your night's fast; boosting your energy levels, metabolism, and alertness; and providing other essential nutrients required for wellness.

What

Breakfast should consist of foods like fruit, oatmeal (without added sugar), Kamut, nuts, blueberries, porridge, and smoothies and should ideally include carbs, proteins, fiber, fats, vitamins, and minerals.

How

Mindful eating involves taking at least half an hour to eat breakfast in a relaxed and restful environment. Digestion is better.

Lunch

Caloric content: 500–700 calories, or 30 percent of your daily food intake

Lunch is usually the second meal of the day. Did you know that lunch became a part of our lifestyles around the seventeenth century? Before that, people didn't eat lunch. Still, there are four things you should be mindful of: when, why, what, and how you eat.

When

You should eat lunch, on average, four hours after breakfast.

Why

You've gone without food for several hours. Your energy may be lagging, making it difficult for you to work and concentrate. Food gives you energy. Eating lunch raises your blood sugar level in the middle of the day, helping you focus for the rest of the afternoon. You eat lunch to reenergize and raise blood sugar levels so you can resume your work.

What

Lunch should consist of foods like a healthy salad with dressing on the side, a sandwich, yogurt, whole grain bread, fruit, and vegetables and should ideally combine complex carbohydrates with lean protein to form a concentrated, long-lasting source of energy.

How

On average, school children take seven to ten minutes to consume their lunches, while most people at work eat lunch in fifteen minutes or less. Ideally, however, you should take at least half an hour to eat lunch in a peaceful and relaxing environment. When you do, you digest your food better. Watching the news or talk shows on your lunch break is not advised.

Dinner

Caloric content: 500–700 calories, or 30 percent of your daily food intake.

This should be your last major meal of the day.

When

Dinner should be eaten between 5:00 p.m. and 7:30 p.m.

Why

Dinnertime used to be family time. Studies indicate that families that sit down to dinner together are more likely to eat a nutritious dinner—for example, fruits and vegetables. In addition, other reports suggest that eating dinner reduces the risk of obesity and cancer and improves energy levels,

What

Dinner should consist of proteins (e.g., beans, nuts, or meat substitutes like garden burgers or tofu), Kamut, vegetables (e.g., broccoli, peppers, greens, tomatoes, or carrots), fruits (e.g., bananas, apples, melons, oranges, or grapes), and grains (e.g., rice, potatoes, pasta, or oats).

How

Take at least half an hour to eat dinner in a calm and relaxing environment. This will help you digest the food. Avoid distractions, such as cellphones, texting, and television—no eating on the run.

Snacks (Optional)

Caloric Content: 150–200 calories, or 20 percent of your daily food intake

When

You may eat one to two snacks per day, based on your activity level. The timing varies, but both midmorning and midafternoon snacks should be spaced two to three hours apart from your main meals (e.g., breakfast at 7 a.m., snack at 10 a.m., and lunch at 12 p.m.).

Why

Snacking means eating or drinking something between meals. The benefits of snacking include providing energy in the middle of the day, decreasing your hunger, stabilizing your glycemic levels, and preventing you from overeating at mealtimes.

What

Snacks should be balanced in terms of their macronutrients and should include 3 grams of fiber, 5–10 grams of protein, and no more than 12 grams of fat. Snacks should consist of foods with plenty of good carbs, dietary fiber, protein, and healthy fats. Examples of healthy snacks include ½ cup of nuts and seeds or a serving of fresh fruit, like apple slices.

How

Snack mindfully. Be aware that you're snacking. Be aware of what you're putting in your mouth and gut. Is it harming or healing you? Refrain from sitting in front of the computer, texting, watching television, or even reading a book while eating so as not to over snack.

There is a time to eat; and a time to stop eating:

Although there is controversy about whether eating late is harmful, few arguments exist over fasting, taking a fast, or break from eating. We do this with break-fast by not eating for 7-8 eights. Think about it. We wouldn't run our cars all day; why do it to the body with food? We should not be eating all day. Experts say our eating activities should end about three hours before bedtime to relax our digestive system. Eating too late and eating large meals harm our health by predisposing us to weight gain and high blood pressure. As we sleep, our heart rates slow down, and so do our digestive systems. Did you know it takes three hours to digest a six-hundred -calorie meal? Some experts even advise that we shut down our eating by 7 p.m.

Insight

Eating is an essential energy generator. In living, energy is required for everything we do. Think of one activity that you do that needs no energy? One place, we obtain energy is food. All food, however, is not equal, with some food being healthy for you and others unhealthy. Although we all have our personal preferences with quantity, time, and taste surrounding food, it's a win-win when we adopt an eating practice that includes healthy foods that align with our circadian rhythms. Doing this helps regulate our metabolism, including blood glucose levels, blood pressure, cholesterol levels, weight, heart vitality, and even stress.

ENJOYABLE, HEALTHY AND HEALING RECIPES

When the diet is wrong, medicine is of no use.
When diet is correct, medicine is no need.
—Ayurvedic Proverb

My recipes largely include measured amounts of olive oil, organic canola oil, avocado oil, and macadamia oil. Vegetables, whole grains, protein, fruit, fats, water, and teas are the foundation for my menu. In cooking, I use a wide variety of spices, such as turmeric, coriander, ground cumin, black cumin seeds, garam masa, sage, bay leaves, oregano, ginger, garlic, cardamom, thyme, anise, cinnamon, nutmeg, paprika, curry powder, black pepper, white pepper, fenugreek, caraway seeds, yellow mustard seeds, black mustard seeds, basil, and fennel seeds.

I drink water with electrolytes, distilled water, or tea. So, there you have it. Over the years, my cooking philosophy has evolved to emphasize living to heal rather than living to eat. When faced with a health challenge, I've resorted to changing my way of living. More than two decades ago, I excluded meat, dairy, fast food, and ultra-processed foods from my diet. Simultaneously, I began practicing mindfulness, energy practices, yoga, qi gong, aromatherapy, gardening, cooking and organic foods, and communing more with nature.

Through my yoga practice, I was introduced to Ayurveda, a healing science originating in ancient India that attends to the body's needs from a constitution perspective to re-balance our lives. Harish Johari writes, "Ayurveda comes from ayu meaning 'life' and 'Veda' meaning 'knowledge.'" Probably, because of my health challenges, I felt a connection with Ayurveda. So, I started cooking in a certain way and including spices for specific therapeutic reasons. Along the way, however, as a consummate seeker of knowledge, I discovered a parallel between Ayurveda and Kemetic lifestyle. In particular, as I studied, I found similarities between the ancient Kemetic diets and Indian cuisine, especially in the use of spices such coriander as a "cooling stimulant" or "carminative." Both also used garlic as a healing elixir for asthma and respiratory diseases.

The more I learned, the more I cooked. Food as medicine fascinated me. Now that I've embraced Ayurveda, spices are no longer just spices but medicine. For example, coriander, saffron, and cumin are cooling and balancing, while turmeric's nature is hot and dry and increases bile. Cooking is no longer simply about slicing and dicing, boiling or baking, sauteing or simmering, tasting and chewing but also about creating and healing. When I cut a carrot, I'm mindful that I'm cutting that carrot. Food holds energy and should be respected. I love to cook, and that love goes into the meal. Often, I've found restaurant food to be too salty, and sometimes not of an optimal quality.

For me, over time that's dangerous, because of the life force inherent in nature, everything we eat either produces a balancing or unbalancing reaction inside our body. Test it. Eat too much salt and sugar and see how you feel. We react based on both the nature of the food and the body's internal and external nature. Although, we're unmindful of what we eat or how it affects our organs, our body isn't. For example, too much sugar distresses the pancreas and weakens the memory. I'm told my food is delicious, light and healthy.

Ayurveda fosters awareness and understanding of our constitutions and the nature of the foods we eat. Whether it's spinach, sweet potatoes, cucumbers, red beets, carrots, tomatoes, bananas, mangos, pineapples, lemons, or grapefruits, food carries not only nutritional values but energetic powers. Conversely, the western delivery of food fails to appreciate the subtle beautiful nature of food, instead we adhere to a one-size-fits-all models. Everyone eats the same food, the same way. As well, if some people are told not eat mushrooms, apples or tomatoes, everyone is warned against it. Not so with Ayurveda, which emphasizes the personalized nature of foods and its interaction on the individual. Food is not generic, but energetically specialized.

That's why, one universal and resounding message in the healing process, whether in ancient Egypt or India, is to know thyself. And know your dosha or temperament: wind (vata), bile (pitta), and mucous (kapha). With this self-knowledge, our journeys become personal rituals for balance, health and healing. What are your rituals?

Dal (Daal)

Ingredients

- ✓ 4 cups cold water
- ✓ 1 cup of split mung beans, washed and drained
- ✓ 2 teaspoons ground coriander
- ✓ 1teaspoon ground turmeric
- ✓ 1 teaspoon Celtic salt

Directions

Bring water to a boil in a heavy stainless-steel pan. Add split mung beans, spices, and salt. Reduce heat to medium. Cover and simmer 45 minutes, or until mung beans are soft and easily mashed with a spoon. Remove from heat and allow to cool 10 minutes.

Variations

Substitute lentils or dried beans for mung beans.

Add zucchini, spinach, chopped broccoli, carrots, green beans, or asparagus.

Benefits

Heart healthy. Rich in iron, potassium, magnesium, and vitamin B, which regulates heart rate and helps to prevent major cardiovascular diseases. Also improves blood circulation throughout the body and regulates blood glucose.

Dandelion Salad with Arugula and Beets

Ingredients

- ✓ 2 cups of fresh-cut organic dandelion greens
- ✓ 1 cup organic arugula washed, dried, and torn
- ✓ 1 teaspoon of black sesame seeds
- ✓ 1 beet, steamed and sliced
- ✓ 1 tomato chopped into small size (optional)
- ✓ 2 teaspoons goji berries (optional)
- ✓ 2 tbs of sesame salad dressing to taste

Directions

In a medium stainless-steel bowl, combine the dandelion greens, arugula, tomatoes, and steamed beets. Sprinkle a few goji berries in your mixture.

Transfer and arrange on a plate.

Put sesame dressing on salad and toss to coat. Serve fresh.

Benefits

Arugula: Cancer-fighting power food rich in chlorophyll. A hydrating leafy green. Good for bone health. Helps reduce inflammation and cleanses and detoxifies the body. Aids in weight loss.

Dandelion- Provide antioxidants, reduce inflammation, manage blood pressure. ... control blood sugar, lower cholesterol.

Beets- Lowered blood pressure, Stamina, Muscle power, Slowed dementia.

Healthy weight, Cancer prevention, Potassium.

These vegetables contain antioxidants and can help fight inflammation, control blood sugar, and reduce cholesterol. Excellent source of vitamins A, C, E, and K and folate and also contains small amounts of other B vitamins. Provides a substantial amount of several minerals, including iron, calcium, magnesium, and potassium.

Raw Kale Salad with Hemp Oil

Ingredients

- ✓ 1 bunch organic lacinato kale
- ✓ 1 teaspoon hemp oil
- ✓ 1 ripe organic avocado
- ✓ 1 teaspoon fresh lemon juice
- ✓ 1/8 teaspoon Celtic alt

Directions

Rinse kale extremely well. Shake leaves dry. Cut into small bite-size pieces.

Place in stainless steel bowl. Rinse again and drain all water.

Pour in hemp oil and mix well.

Using your hands, massage cut avocados into kale. Add lemon juice and blend.

Sprinkle with Celtic salt.

Optional: Add walnuts, blanched almonds, or pistachios.

Benefits

Kale: Contains powerful antioxidants, like quercetin and kaempferol. Lowers cholesterol, which may reduce the risk of heart disease. One of the best sources of vitamin K and cancer-fighting Substances.

Hemp Oil: Treats inflammation, anxiety, and pain, boosts the immune system, improves digestive health, and promotes a healthy brain and heart.

Celtic Sea Salt*: Provides trace minerals and vitamin.

*Consuming too much sodium is linked to negative health outcomes.

Pan-Seared* Sprouted Tofu

Ingredients

- ✓ 16 oz. organic sprouted high protein tofu, super firm, drained and rinsed
- ✓ 2 tablespoons canola oil
- ✓ Jollof seasoning to taste

Directions

Squeeze and pat tofu dry with paper towels to remove excess water. You can use a tofu press or two plates to drain excess water from tofu.

Cut into triangles about 1-inch thick. Season with jollof seasoning.

Heat a large cast iron skillet over high heat. Add oil. Once oil is hot, carefully add tofu in a single layer. Sear each side for 1-2 minutes, or until sides are golden and crisped. Drain on paper towels.

Jollof Seasoning Recipe

1½ ground ginger, 1 tsp garlic powder, 2 tsp dried chili flakes, 1 heaped tsp dried thyme, 1 generous tsp ground cinnamon, ½ tsp ground nutmeg, 1 tsp ground coriander, 1 pinch of Celtic salt, 1 pinch of ground black pepper.

Mix ingredients in a bowl. Store in a sealed container in a cool, dark place and use within a few months.

Benefits

Vegan protein with complete essential amino acids. Contains key micronutrients, like manganese, calcium, and selenium.

*Pan searing is a cooking technique used in which the surface of the food is cooked at a high temperature until a browned crust form.

Forbidden Rice (Purple Rice)

Ingredients

- ✓ 1 cup rice
- ✓ 2 cups water

Directions

Bring water to boil and rice to a boil, let simmer uncovered until tender about 30 minutes. Do not disturb while simmering. Drain and fluff.

Remove rice from heat. Let sit covered another 10 minutes to steam before serving.

Benefits

Contains high levels of seven different anthocyanin polyphenols—a type of flavonoid that has antioxidant benefits. Powerful Antioxidant, Lowers Cholesterol, Fights Cancer, Anti-inflammatory, Promotes Healthy Weight Management, and Promotes Healthy Brain Function.

- Black rice – 200 calories | 34 g carbs| 6 grams protein |

Quinoa

Ingredients

- ✓ 1 cup red quinoa
- ✓ 1½ cups water or broth

Directions

Rinse quinoa to remove any bitterness caused by naturally occurring saponins, which are produced by the plants to ward off pests.

Combine rinsed quinoa and water or broth in a medium saucepan. Bring to a boil.

Reduce heat to low and cover. Simmer until tender and most of the liquid has been absorbed, 10 to 15 minutes.

Remove pot from heat and let quinoa steam covered for 5 minutes.

Fluff quinoa and serve.

Variations

Add carrots, mushrooms, fresh spinach, seeded tomatoes, or minced fresh onions.

Benefits

A superfood. Gluten-free, high in protein, and one of the few plant foods that contain sufficient amounts of all nine essential amino acids.

Navy Bean Soup

Preparation time with pressure cooker: about 1 hour plus overnight soak Preparation time without pressure cooker: 2-3 hours plus overnight soak

Ingredients

- ✓ 3 cups organic dried navy beans, sorted and soaked overnight*
- ✓ 5 stalks celery,finely chopped
- ✓ 3 cloves garlic, minced
- ✓ 1 green pepper, cut into small pieces
- ✓ 1 onion, diced
- ✓ 1 stick of kombu (a sea vegetable)
- ✓ 1/8 teaspoon Hing
- ✓ 2 teaspoon coriander
- ✓ 2 teaspoons sage
- ✓ 1 teaspoon Celtic salt
- ✓ 8 cups water, or enough to cover beans and vegetables
- ✓ 2 tablespoons organic tomato paste (optional)
- ✓ brown rice for serving (optional)

Directions

Rinse-soaked beans overnight to lessen any gas potential. Drain completely.

Add beans, chopped vegetables, Hing, kombu and other seasoning to a large pot. Add water to pot and bring to a boil.

Add the onions, celery, garlic and green pepper.

Reduce heat to medium and cook until beans are soft and mash easily

Cook for 2-3 hours. Stir well.

Add more water to thin, if needed. Add tomato paste, if using. Stir and simmer 15 minutes.

Eat as single soup or serve with brown rice.

Benefits

A good source of protein and complex carbohydrates (from navy beans). Lowers risk of diabetes. High in fiber and resistant starch. Supports heart health and improves memory and cognition. Promotes muscle growth and repair, aids in weight loss and reduces risk of cancer.

*Some bags of navy beans may be old and take longer to soften, so be patient because your beans may take longer to cook.

TIME FOR TEA: ÀSET TEA ROOM

The Path to Heaven Passes through a teapot
Ancient Proverb

For me, tea is not merely a tea bag; it is an inspiring elixir. I confess, I am a tea lover. The entire experience ritual of drinking tea is a highly anticipated process for me. Tea has been not only good to me but also *for* me. When I drink tea, I feel relaxed and at peace. As a child, I remember serving imaginary tea and even then, forgetting whatever was bothering me. Later, I found enjoyment in drinking tea, purchasing beautiful teacups, using only the best water, and taking care to acquaint myself with the needs of the tea leaves. And then, I did the unbelievable: I opened the Àset Tearoom with the intention of introducing others to the relaxing nature of tea. I enjoy serving tea but also indulging in it.

What is tea? This is what I've learned that tea is a plant rich in flavonoids, fluorine, and polyphenols and contains a vasodilator, which prevents the muscles from tightening and the walls from narrowing. As a result, blood flows more easily through vessels, and the heart doesn't have to pump as hard, reducing blood pressure. Tea comes from the leaves of the *Camellia sinensis* plant. This tea plant of these four variations black, green, white, or oolong. Black and green teas appear to be favorites in the United States.

Many stories exist surrounding the origin of tea, but Southwest China is considered the birthplace. Today, however, tea is produced in other places, including Africa, South America, and the area around the Black and Caspian Seas. Below is a few of my favorite teas.

Pu-erh or Pu er Tea

Pu-erh tea would make a coffee drinker shout for joy because it is so delicious. This is a semifermented "dark tea," or black tea, from the Yunnan province of China. Pu-erh goes through microbial fermentation after the tea leaves have been thoroughly dried and rolled. I drink shou Pu-erh, which is ripened and contains beneficial fungi and bacteria. The taste is intense, earthy, savory, and smoky. Pu-erh is an acquired taste, but I find most coffee drinkers enjoy it. It is good for digestion, lowers cholesterol, and promotes the breakdown of greasy food.

Chai

Chai is a blend of tea and spices. I've made tea in a big pot and found it amazing. My chai includes organic black tea, cardamom, cinnamon, ginger root, star anise, black pepper, nutmeg, and cloves. Chai will lift your spirits.

I use a nondairy creamer with 0.5 grams of fat and no cholesterol. It is carrageenan free, soy free, and gluten free and contains no preservatives.

Purple Tea

Purple tea is a recent discovery for me. While most teas are from China, India, Tibet, or Japan, this tea is grown in Kenya. It is the only known tea plant to contain anthocyanin, the flavonoid responsible for giving blueberries and pomegranates their purplish color. Although the leaves start green, they turn to a purple hue as they mature. Purple tea is low in caffeine, containing less than green tea but slightly more than white tea).

Black Tea

Black tea comes from the *Camellia sinensis* var. *assamica,* a larger-leafed tea plant. During the cultivating process, the tea leaves become fully oxidized before being heat-processed and dried. Oxidation occurs when oxygen interacts with the tea plant's cell walls to turn the leaves a rich dark brown or even black. Black tea goes through a laborious oxidation process to bring forth a smooth, smoky, soothing taste.

Green Tea

Green tea comes from the Camellia Sinensis or tea tree; however, leaves and buds have not undergone the same withering and oxidation process used to make oolong and black teas. Dehydration occurs with the leaves and buds of green teas to prevent any possible oxidation, increasing the plant leaves' greenness. There are more than 1,500 varieties of green tea leaves.

◆ ◆ ◆

In making tea, there are four important points to consider: the quality of the tea leaves, the temperature and quality of the water, the method you use, and for me, the quality of your tea container (i.e., cup).

The quality of tea is determined by its age, region, and processing method. I prefer loose-leaf teas that are organic and fair trade and are sourced from reliable tea dealers. The exact water temperature for tea leaves is critical. Black, oolong, white, and green teas all require different temperatures. Often, I see people use boiling water for all teas, when brewing green or semifermented teas in 212°F water destroys the flavor of the tea. The ideal brewing temperature of green is 160–170°F. Pour water as soon as it is properly heated. Finally, for me, what I pour my tea into is important. High-quality, beautiful cups add to the flavor and medicinal power of the tea.

Purified water is considered preferable to distilled or filtered water in brewing tea because of its perfect pH level of 7. Next best would be filtered water.

Again, these are only a sample of the teas that I have explored.

Visit the **Àset Tea Room** and start your personal exploration of some of the finest teas, perfectly brewed with the right water at the right temperature, paired with the healthiest vegan foods. Here's to: "Chado," means "the way of tea."

Drinking a daily cup of tea will surely starve the apothecary.
~Chinese Proverb

SELF-CARE

The physical body is not something
separate from our mind and soul.
—B. K. S. Iyengar

Self-care is the highest form of self-love. Self-Care is the precursor to health care. Environment, mental and physical toxicities, eating habits, and the way we live can cause irreparable damage because we neglect to care for ourselves. As a result of this environmental, physical, and psychological toxicity, our bodies become sluggish, dis-eased, and imbalanced. Moreover, our unhealthy eating habits and lifestyle choices is an abandonment of the Self.

Healthiness is a practice. It entails sustainability and is a 24/7 commitment. It's not enough to go away to a retreat to come back and continue unhealthy eating when you return. To reconnect with health, at Àse Yoga, we begin with an intention; seasonally, we eat a mono-diet of organ-targeted Kitchardi and salad, drink water, and potassium broth, meditate, and practice yoga. In addition, we eliminate certain items during this time. Our results have been weight loss, mindfulness, weaning away from harmful elements, and enhanced willpower to live to heal.

Our Intention
• remove impurities • renew our bodies, minds, and spirits • support healthy digestive and elimination systems • restore energy • healing

What we Eat (Mono-Diet)
• Fresh fruits and vegetables • Kitchardi (good for the digestive system, lungs, and kidneys) • detoxifying adzuki beans

What We Drink
• potassium broth • herbal, noncaffeinated teas • water

What We Eliminate
• added sugar • added salt • saturated fat • trans fat • alcohol • refined carbs • red meat • MSG • dairy products • caffeine • artificial sweetener

Wellness Reset
• Meditate • Reset our breathing • Practice Àse yoga • Massages • Journal • Retreat

Our Results over the Past Fifteen Year

✓ Normalization of blood pressure
✓ Weight Loss
✓ Reduction of cholesterol levels
✓ Decrease in visceral fat
✓ Decrease in body fat
✓ Glucose brought within normal range
✓ Regular bowel movements
✓ Feeling Good
✓ Clarity

SELF CARE CHECK LIST

DIET
- ☐ More Fiber
- ☐ More Fruit
- ☐ More Vegetables
- ☐ More Water

DIET
- ☐ Less Sugar
- ☐ Less Salt
- ☐ Less Soda & Alcohol
- ☐ Less Saturated Fat

LIFESTYLE
- ☐ More Sleep
- ☐ More Nature
- ☐ More Exercise
- ☐ More Traveling
- ☐ More Friendships
- ☐ More Health Awareness
- ☐ More Time w/ Family
- ☐ More Reading
- ☐ More Goals / Purpose
- ☐ More Wealth Creation

LIFESTYLE
- ☐ Less Self-Comparison / Less Social Media
- ☐ Less Negative Self Talk
- ☐ Less Disorganization
- ☐ Less Mindless Spending
- ☐ Less Smoking / Vaping
- ☐ Less Drugs, Painkillers, Artificial Stimulants
- ☐ Less Arguments
- ☐ Less Self Avoidance

CONNECTION
- ☐ More Positive Interactions
- ☐ More Connections with Neighbors
- ☐ More Involvement in Community
- ☐ More Learning & Teaching Others
- ☐ More Civil Engagement
- ☐ More Cultural Exposure
- ☐ More Patience w/ Change
- ☐ More Life

CONNECTION
- ☐ Less Isolation
- ☐ Less Anger
- ☐ Less Resentment
- ☐ Less Fear & Judgement
- ☐ Less Aggression & Violence
- ☐ Less Deception, Manipulation
- ☐ Less Conflict & Misunderstanding
- ☐ Less Death

PERSONAL REVELATIONS

Personal revelation is the way we know for
ourselves the most important truth of existence.
Robert D. Hales

Understanding: Lao Tzu says that once a matter becomes clear, there is nothing more to be done, for then the understanding leads all our actions and makes us do what is worth doing. Understanding is everything, and understanding is enough. If our relationships with food is to change, we must comprehend what food means to us and what messages we are sending out surrounding food. Do we eat for survival or recreation? Is our eating motivated by our environments or emotions, such as love or pain? It's not enough to occasionally diet without understanding why we eat the way we do. When the why becomes clear, the path becomes clear for us to experience sustainable health.

Conversely, when we don't understand, nothing we do sustains itself. We ingest unhealthy foods, load up on saturated fats, overindulge in sweet and salty entrees, and gulp our meals rather than savor them. Our food routine stays the same. Even if we diet or decide on surgical weight loss, it means nothing; the relapse is sure to come. This goes for the nearly 11 million people suffering from food-related ailments every year; health is an issue of understanding. Lack of understanding is perhaps why as many as 80 to 95 percent of dieters gain back the weight they've lost. Understanding is transformative. Open yourself to health and healing. Take a moment to reflect on what you're feeding yourself by understanding your food story. I did and it change my life.

Letting Go of Emotional Clutter:

When we carry something too long, we forget that we're carrying it after a while. The same goes for anger, grief, anxiety, low self-esteem, frustration, misery, nervousness, oppression, disappointment, awkwardness, confusion, craving, disgust, egotism, and fear. These emotions become overlooked until we pause to take inventory of what we're lugging around. When we do, we might take some stuff out or let go. Underlining our unhealthiness are emotions that need understanding and release. Let me give you an example. Say you get married, but it ends in divorce. Amid your emotional distress, you neglect to care for yourself. You find yourself overeating or, as someone said, "doing that crazy eating" because of unhappiness over the divorce. Delving more deeply, you might find that you got married to hide your prior emotional clutter. Perhaps marriage served as a shield or an escape from feelings of low self-esteem, fulfillment of your parents' wishes, or masked your childhood insecurities and trauma?. Disposing of emotional clutter is a two-step process. First, we understand to be able to see the emotions. Second, we commit to healing and let go of feelings, thoughts, and behaviors we no longer need. Before letting go, we must understand our food stories, that is why we eat and what we eat, and our way of life to release emotions, thoughts, and behaviors that interfere with our healing journeys. Neither process is easy because our minds cling to the familiar and thus put-up resistance against change. For example, in understanding and letting go, we may hear excuses like "I'll do it later," "this juice doesn't have too much sugar," or "I just need to get to the gym." Our mind sabotages our innate right to healthiness by justifying why we do what we do, even if it's unhealthy. Until we let go of our emotional clutter, we'll continue a way of life that neglects our most precious asset: ourselves.

Recondition Ourselves

Re-" means back. "Condition" means learning. We have to re-learn ways to take care of ourselves. Our food conditioning either promotes healthiness or unhealthiness. The key to health is reconditioning our physical and mental habits. To do that, we must understand that to mitigate food-related diseases such as obesity, type 2 diabetes, high cholesterol, some types of cancer, Alzheimer's disease, and cardiovascular, liver, and kidney diseases, we must substitute healthy responses for unhealthy responses. Before we replace them, however, we must know or assess what's going on in our lives. Is something bothering us? Awareness of the truth behind what we're doing is imperative. I checked my glucose twice a day for ninety days to determine my pattern or trend because I came from a diabetic family lineage and wanted to be mindful of that truth. At the end of the test period, my average glucose level was 100, which equaled 5.1 AC1 levels. Knowing that information, I refrained from eating diabetes-triggering foods such as white grains, sugary drinks, fast food, and pasta. Because I came from a gene pool that was prone to diabetes, I wanted to change my unconscious conditioning, knowing that it influenced my life choices. We are our conditioning. Sadly, too many of us don't make an effort, give up, or feel powerless to change the unhealthy ways we've learned to do something as essential as eating or taking care of ourselves. But why not make our time on earth, one of health and healing rather than illness and disease. Let's recondition ourselves to share our healing and not our diseases.

A Spiritual Practice: Health is not just about the mental, physical, material, or even the vital signs:

- Body temperature.
- Pulse rate.
- Respiration rate (rate of breathing)
- Blood pressure (Blood pressure is not considered a vital sign but is often measured along with the vital signs.)
- Height
- Weight
- Oxygen saturation (SpO2)

A spiritual practice, however, is also part of health. Setting aside time for a spiritual practice such as meditation, breathing, relaxation, yoga, or qigong; attending church, the mosque, or the temple does our bodies and minds well. While a spiritual practice may sound overwhelming and abstruse, adhering to spiritual practice has been a lifesaver for me. I wouldn't be here without it. Of course, like others, I'm challenged on some days more than on others, but I'm never discouraged. I make time for prayers, meditation, and spiritual readings to nourish my soul. My spiritual practice reminds me to live every moment, be in the present moment, take care of myself, express gratitude, and fulfill my purpose. Maintaining unhealthy relationships and lifestyles is no different from eating junk food; both lack nutritional value

Over the years, I watched and listened to people overlook the need for spiritual practice. They engage in other behaviors like vaping, smoking, and even escapism. Even though they utter statements like "I'm not doing well," or "I feel like something is wrong with me," - their response doesn't change. When you look at their behavior, you realize they've become used to responding in this heighten fight-flight way and thus avoid other ways such as meditating, progressive relaxation techniques, or even slow breathing. Instead, they ruminate, overthink the crisis, the situation, rarely changing their stress response to a relaxation one. We all claim stress, uncertainties, busy schedules, lack of energy, exhaustion, and insufficient time but how we respond is the key.

Experiencing the same situations, complaining about our plight in life, and entertaining chronic stress reveal spiritual deficiencies. Some of this comes from spending time on social media, watching cable news, late-night pundits, binge-watching television, and playing video games. These activities may trigger us to eat more, eat unhealthily, feel anxious, and feel stressed. However, when we connect with a spiritual practice, life takes on new meaning with purpose at the forefront. We become conscious of why we're living and transforming becomes a natural occurrence. Clarity replaces confusion, inspiration replaces fear, and health replaces diseases. Integral to health and healing is a spiritual practice. However, what we do with our twenty-four hours, seven days a week enhances or exacerbates our situations. If we allocate some moments in our day, week, and life to be well and be better human beings, life in kind will respond favorably.

Breathe: Whenever I find myself stressed or overwhelmed, I check my breathing. We underestimate the power of our breath. But where the mind goes, the breath goes. If our mind is in chaos, our breathing will be too. You're probably thinking "I, know how to breathe." I did think that, too, until I realized I didn't know. I've spent most of my life unconsciously inhaling and exhaling in a way that has wreaked havoc on my body and mind. The way I was using my nearly 21,000 daily breaths routinely activated my stress response, or fight-or-flight sympathetic nervous system. Breathing this way quickened my pulse while releasing cortisol and other hormones into my body. It also resulted in chronic digestive problems, such as constipation, belly pain, and occasional appetite loss. I know I am not alone. Those ailments continued until I learned to breathe.

Indeed, breathing incorrectly took its toll on me. My awareness of the breath came from my yoga practice. That changed when I discovered breathing was natural but also conditioned or learned. I'd learn to breathe incompletely because of my childhood experiences. Unresolved emotions had cut short my life force. With practice, I began experiencing the effect of long, slow, deep breaths cascading through my body- breath, by breath, and I felt years of confusion and conflict leave as I exhaled. Instantly, I realized that one of the greatest gifts we can give ourselves is learning to breathe. When we do, we optimize the oxygen in our digestive system, decrease our heart rates, and release 70 percent of the toxins in our bodies. Inhaling a long, slow, and deep breath into the diaphragm, followed by a complete exhale, we activate the "rest and digest" response, which relaxes us, improves our digestion, and reduces blood pressure and anxiety. Focus and breathe to *Wellness Begins Inside.*

"Some of us are overweight on the outside, yet most of us are overweight on the inside." Dr. Alston

C.U.P WAY

Each moment I am alive becomes a realization
that every discomfort, disease, and disappointment
I experience is an opportunity for me to
understand, transcend, and heal. —Dr. Alston

C.U.P. Mindset

After enduring years of feeling powerlessness regarding my health and being overly reliant on the medical, not health system, I decided to stop doing what was harming me. Prevention seemed far more attractive than intervention. Meanwhile, the question that came to me was *how* I was contributing to my suffering or ill-health? That humble inquiry became the driving force behind *Wellness Begins Inside*. Experiences, inquiry, and suffering brought forth a novel mindset flowing from my revelations that brought forth three concepts: Consciousness, Understanding, and Purpose, or the C.U.P. mindset.

Consciousness simply means to be aware. Simple does not imply easy, because it isn't. Often, we're not mindful of our health until something threatens it, and sometimes not even then. We're on automatic pilot, wherein we act "without a conscious intention or an awareness of our present-moment sensory perception." And so, we go through life unconscious of the damage we're inflicting by the habitual overeating of unhealthy foods. Even ingesting negative thoughts and consuming toxicity takes a toll on our health. What wakes us up? Sometimes the way we look, excessive weight, dis-eases, and death of family or friend. At that moment, consciousness compels us to engage in self-inquiry to understand our experiences in new ways and ultimately develop healthy behaviors. We ask ourselves, what am I doing? In answering that question, we bring to the forefront everything that has been holding us back from being healthy. As a mindset, C.U.P. re-shapes our way of thinking to generate life-affirming actions. When that happens, we no longer unconsciously harm ourselves; we heal. Healing is not magical; it's a conscious practice wherein we re-engineer our thoughts towards wellnesses. This emerging *consciousness* brings forth the energy of aliveness with personal responsibility to be healthy.

Another principle is *understanding* our food stories which links us back to our consciousness. Several times throughout this book, I've evoked the power of understanding. Admittedly, I did not understand why I ate the way I did or the reasoning behind what I ate. It didn't matter until I witnessed the carnage among family, friends, and myself. They say when you know better, you do better. Perhaps, it's not knowing but understanding that makes our life better. Nothing changes without consciousness and understanding; our food story stays the same, and we continue to play a game of chance with health. Occasionally, we hear about a diet or someone's miraculous weight loss, and we join it. Still, if misunderstanding is present, our results will be temporary, short-lived, or unsuccessful. How do we understand something we're unaware of? The most we'll do is talk about what we want to do, even though this talk falls short of action. For example, we continue overindulging in ice cream, eggnog, pizza, chemically and ultra-processed foods high in saturated fats, and other salty and sugary foods. Unhealthiness represents a misunderstanding that is reflected by the choices we make. At the same time, healthiness arises from our own consciousness and understanding. When we understand, our actions reflect that understanding by changing our choices in food and the way we live. *Understanding* gives us the added momentum to act with consciousness.

Early on in my life, I moved about aimlessly and unconsciously, doing whatever was presented to me without any thought. I really didn't connect with purpose other than to fulfill other people's desires. Yet, life-threatening challenges awoke me to my purpose. What happened next was, as Sa'di says, "Every soul is created for a certain purpose, and the light of that purpose has been kindled in that soul." The light of my purpose rekindled my soul. I left a job that was not my purpose to pursue what was. A weight lifted off me at that moment, and my eyes became clear. Drudgery and fear faded away. We've forgotten our purpose or never realized it and thus disconnect from the meaning of life. Without purpose, we do anything, eat mindlessly and carelessly because we fail to see the connection. However, connecting with purpose changes our lives. Suffice to say that every person has a purpose in life that, when discovered, flowers us into healthy and healing beings.

With this mindset —consciousness, understanding, and purpose—we forge a different connection with food, eating, and living. And so, in *Live, Beloved Live*, the C.U.P. prescription is sure to transform your life.

Watermelon Radish

REFLECTIONS

Every one of us has a story that we share, a message that we deliver to ourselves, and to everyone and everything around us.
—Don Miguel Ruiz and Don Jose Ruiz

Are you healthy?

Health has been mentioned one hundred and eighty-one times in this book. But what is it? We know sickness and disease, but what about health? Have you ever been sick? In the hospital, emergency room? Was it an accident or a chronic disease? Have you been diagnosed with a disease? Does health mean the absence of physical disease? Or that our blood work fell within the acceptable ranges for cholesterol, glucose, white blood cell count levels, and blood pressure? Can a depressed person be healthy? Does health include our psychological and spiritual state? According to the World Health Organization (WHO) and the Centers for Disease

Control (C.D.C.), health is a state of *complete* physical, mental, and social well-being and not merely the absence of disease or infirmity. So, if health is not simply the absence of disease, what is it? According to Chinese Medicine, health is the balance in Qi or life force. Any imbalance to Qi can cause disease and illness. This imbalance is most commonly thought to be caused by an alteration in the opposite and complementary forces within the macrocosm (universe) and microcosm (human body). In traditional Chinese Medicine, good health is achieved by various balances between yin and yang. According to John Hopkins Medicine, Chinese Medicine seeks to "restore the body's balance and harmony between the natural opposing forces of yin and yang, which can block qi and cause disease."

In Yoga & Ayurveda, Dr. Frawley writes that health includes "not only physical health but also mental preparation for the spiritual life. Health is defined as a "balance in bodily systems and uses diet, herbal treatment, and yogic breathing and lifestyle." another health explanation for more than three thousand years in Ayurveda is India's traditional medicinal medical system. Going even further back to another ancient health system, African traditional Medicine, "Good health for the African consists of mental, physical, spiritual, and emotional stability oneself, family members, and community." Omonzejele 2008:120)." Thus, health is "not just about the proper functioning of bodily organs but includes the spiritual, mental, and emotional stability [of oneself, family members, and community]." Moreover, the therapeutic system of Ancient Egypt, one of the earliest recorded medical treatment systems, spanning more than two thousand years, offers the following health formula: diet and herbs and a spiritual prescription of prayer, mantras, hekau (words of power), and even meditation.

As you can see, the practice of health is ancient, and when we look deeper, we'll see it goes beyond the body and even the mind into the soul. Fortunately, through their experiences, our ancestors passed down to us a blueprint for healthiness that is spiritual and communal. Health is not just what we eat but a way of life but through interconnectedness, with the cosmos, spirituality, nature, energy, and even relationships with God, our ancestors, and the universe. Are you healthy?

Healing

One of the ways we heal is with soul food. Foods to rejuvenate and support wellness. Soul food possesses medicinal and energetic properties to balance and counteract certain illnesses or imbalances. For example, some of us eat chicken noodle soup for a cold; use garlic or ginger as antibiotics, and consume dark, leafy vegetables as antioxidants. We also use mushrooms to boost our immune system and green tea to reduce inflammation. With the availability of more than thirty food documentaries, such as *Cowspiracy: The Sustainability Secret, Food, Inc, Soul Food Junkies, Forks over Knives, Super-Size Me,* and *Food, Inc.*, there is ample evidence that the healing power of food exists. And while food is healing, not everything we eat is food. According to (Encyclopedia Britannica, 2020), "**Food** is a substance consisting essentially of protein, carbohydrate, fats, and other nutrients used in the body of an organism to sustain growth and vital processes and to furnish energy." So, if it lacks nutrition and doesn't maintain life or growth, it's not food.

Soul food is intrinsically healing. I've experienced the healing effects of foods such as garlic as an antibiotic, ginger to settle my stomach, and potassium broth during my seasonal detoxing. We heal with the right mental and spiritual food. Our thoughts and understanding of life can either facilitate healing or obstruct it. Spending too much time worrying, negativity, anger, anxiety, and depression blocks our ability to be well. However, clarity, understanding, and awareness support our quest to be well. Essentially, a spiritual practice changes the way we think and opens us to the possibility of becoming mindful not only of physical food but also of mental and spiritual nourishment.

Happiness

If we're healthy and healing, then are we happy? Does food or the way we live engender happiness? Is the fountain of happiness found in food or the way we live? When we eat, do we feel good? Of course, happiness is a personal experience that varies from individual to individual. But certain foods have the distinction of being associated with happiness—foods such as sugar, salt, and fat. Supposedly, these foods trigger the release of key "pleasure" neurotransmitters. We even have Happy Meals that include a hamburger, cheeseburger, or small order of Chicken McNuggets; a side of French fries or a package of apple slices; a drink of milk, juice, or soda; and a toy. But do these so-called "happy" or "comfort" foods make us happy or sick? Or are they really more about pleasure and satisfaction and less happiness? With 220 million Happy Meals sold each year in the United States, we should be witnessing a lot of happiness. Of course, that's not happening. What we eat may be having a similar effect on us as alcohol by triggering the release of endorphins—chemicals that produce feelings of temporary pleasure—in specific regions of the brain.? When we are unhappy, we feed the unhappiness by chasing after that food-induced happy feeling. We call a Happy Meal with the toy or your happy adult meal with a small glass of vodka none other than a pleasure meal. The real Happy foods that usher forth health and healing include fruits and vegetables, enlightened thoughts, and a way of life.

BE WELL

"Pay attention to what you're giving your body to eat.
Pay attention to what you're giving your mind to eat."
—Shi Heng Yi

Health is a birthright-—claim it. Beloved, become healthy for yourself, your family, and your friends; do it for every cell and organ in your body, and do it for the ancestors who sacrificed for you. Since our health is not fixed, it's changeable or constantly in flux, it's requires round the clock awareness. To become aware is to understand which gradually changes our actions.

A lot of answers are floating around surrounding physical as well as mental health, but often it's for other people, not us. People in the wellness community are guilty of attempting to fix other people lives, while neglecting their own. And yet, none of us are exempted from suffering, diseases and hardships. I remember one year participating in the breast cancer race for the cure for others and being diagnosed with breast cancer the following year. Little did I know I was racing for myself. As young person, I could *care less* about my health. Neither did anyone talk to me about health. Only later in life would I discover that what we do when we're younger affects our bodies later in life. Dis-eases don't just happen; they're, at times, a culminative effect to the way we've been living.

Later, when I was diagnosed with dis-eases, feeling helpless, I surrendered. In hindsight, I grew up knowing my diseases better than the alphabet. Similarly, to many people, disease talk occupied a lot of my conversations. Many of us spend hours talking about our chronic diseases, like arthritis, lupus, asthma, allergies, cancer, chronic obstructive pulmonary disease (COPD), diabetes, gastrointestinal ailments, obesity, headaches, hypertension, autoimmune disorders, depression, and anxiety, yet delay our healing. We say we want to healthy, but we continue our unhealthy lifestyle. Instead, we've become allies with our diseases while dutifully filling one or more of the over 20,000 prescriptions. We affirm our sicknesses while crushing any hopes of wellness. For me, that would all change when my life was threaten. Rather than continue nursing disease, I took up the challenge of pursuing health and healing.

Do you want to live? Do you want to be well? If so, make health a priority. To most of us, losing weight is the only time we pay attention to our health. Over the years, I've heard my fair share of stories about the latest miracle diets. And I've even witnessed instant weight loss from event-orientated gastric bypass surgery in some people. I've also seen enough people go on and off diets yet remain unhealthy. However, dieting is a not a panacea for wellness.

Still, at our disposal is an abundance of diet plans to fulfill our insatiable appetite for losing weight quickly at various times of the year and for specific occasions. At last count, over nine major diet concepts and counting existed for losing weight, including Paleo, Keto, low fat, and low- carbs diets, and so on. Yet, despite our affinity for diets and losing weight, the latest miracle weight-loss program- we're not losing weight. Obesity, which is on the rise, reigns as a leading cause of death, with two out of three Americans identified as overweight.

The National Center for Health Statistics estimates that for the 2017 – 2018 period in the U.S., 42.4% of adults age twenty and over were obese. From 1999 –to 2000 through 2017 –to 2018, U.S. obesity prevalence increased from 30.5% to 42.4%. But obesity may be a symptom, not the cause of our ill-health. That's why, *Wellness Begins Inside* goes beyond our fixation on losing weight to healing as a lifestyle.

Obesity is not our only or main health problem. We're also suffering from a high rate of heart disease, as detected in our LDL, HDL, and Triglycerides tests or Lipid panel and cardiovascular reports. According to the Centers for Disease Control and Prevention (CDC), heart disease remains a leading cause of death in the U.S. Obesity and cardiovascular diseases are happening even though we have more access to health information, books, and even gyms, numerous diet plans, fitness experts, documentary and scientific data. So, what is going on? What are we not doing?

Many people are succumbing to the pitfalls of an unhealthy lifestyle. They feel a sense of helplessness or powerlessness over their health. While others, however, are taking charge of their health by changing their way of living to change their lab tests results such as AIC levels, glucose, cholesterol, and others. Some no longer consume meat or wheat, avoid lectins, and refrain from eating cooked food, eggs, tomatoes, and even exercise. If I could count the number of people who tell me they've stopped eating meat, I'd be richer than Musk. Meanwhile, there is no shortage of books, documentaries, information, and science affirming the benefits of plant-based eating and its impressive effect on our health, so I will not burden you with more. But I assure you there is more to health than dieting or refraining from meat.

Consider this; some non-meat eaters consume various bad carbs from sweets, sweetened beverages, refined grains, and saturated fat from alternative meat products while boldly proclaiming their non-meat dietary status. This lack of meat sometimes is replaced by pastries, cakes, candy, sweet stuff, pasta, potatoes, processed alternative products— no meat, but no vegetables either. And while a few non-meat eaters proudly broadcast at gatherings, "I don't eat meat, "along with an attitude of food superiority over omnivores, health is not defined by the absence of meat on our plates.

By all means, go meatless if you choose, but unhealthiness is not exclusive to those that eat meat, nor is it just about food. Whether we clog our arteries with beef or non-meat-engineered saturated fats, the body reacts the same. To appeal to meat-eaters, even some vegetarian restaurants serve the same unhealthy version of fast foods, as their meat-serving counterparts, just without the meat. Non-meat-eaters are not necessarily plant-based eaters. Also, often, these non-meat eaters are not eating foods with high amounts of fruits, vegetables, whole grains, nuts, or legumes and, thus, are not fully benefitting from the exclusion of meat.

We see these concepts illustrated in this study published in 2002 on eating habits and heart disease among more than 2,000 adults who ate plant-based versus animal-based foods. The results found, for instance, that those who ate more plant-based foods had a risk of heart disease n 11 to –25 percent% lower heart disease risk than that meat-eaters. Another aspect of this study was that that study also highlighted the differences between those who ate healthy plant-based foods and those who ate more unhealthy plant-based meat foods.

The researchers also found that only the participants who followed a healthful plant-based diet—and only them they—had a significantly reduced risk of cardiovascular disease. A considerable reduction in heart disease risk was evident in those who ate healthy plant-based foods. The operative term here is "healthy." "Simply following a plant-based diet is not enough to reduce cardiovascular disease risk," lead author Demosthenes Panagiotakos said. "It is also important to focus on specific, healthful plant-based food groups to see a benefit in terms of reducing cardiovascular disease."

What this suggests is that healthiness is the inclusion of vegetables and fruit. However, eliminating meat but including fruits and vegetables is only part of the health equation. I've known people in their nineties —and even met one centenarian —whose diets include small amounts of animal products. They still appear to be in relatively good health with no cardiovascular challenges. Conversely, I've also known non-meat eaters who did not live beyond seventy-five. Of course, this observation is anecdotal, not a study, but it is relevant. Is there something else related to being healthy?

As a vegan, and yogi, I've learned that optimum health includes food for the body as well as for the mind and spirit. *We have to heal our wounds to experience health. Wellness Begins Inside* believes that involves understanding our food stories. Because in doing so, we become aware of our feelings and emotions driving our actions. Feelings are how we respond to our life experiences. They include emotions such as happiness and sadness, contentment and disappointment, hopefulness or hopelessness, satisfaction or dissatisfaction, courage or fear, peace or anger regarding our life experiences. Our fate in life rest in the hands of our feelings. And so, dealing with our feelings, we uncover the wounds they encase.

An African proverb says this best: "You have to heal the

wound before it ignores the medicine." When my brother died while holding my hand, he had not healed; his wounds were festering, ignoring the medicine. I was hopeful that he, too, would change. Soon, however, hope morphed into hopelessness. His feeling was the driving force for his unresolved childhood emotions, causing his traumatic experiences to ravish his vital organs. Instead of healing, he clung to feelings of abuse, abandonment, stress, depression, infidelity, disappointment, and grief by overdosing on sweet, salty, and crunchy foods. His feelings imprison him with comments such as, "I like it," referring to how he ate. Ultimately, my brother was buried with the feelings and wounds that go with not ever healing.

My brother and I come from humble and impoverished beginnings. Our mother died by the time I was two; my father and siblings died early in their lives. The difference is my determination to heal my wounds by opening up to my feelings, understanding my experiences, and connecting with a spiritual practice. I believe life put me in a situation to heal and share that healing. To do that, I changed my physical nourishment as well as consumed spiritual food, including yoga, qi gong, meditation, breathing, exercising, and energetic practices. Healing became an intention.

I divorce myself from thoughts, actions, and feelings that sustain my unhealthiness. Understanding my food stories became instrumental, and where I discovered that our health challenges are not merely about food but our interpretation of our life experiences. With determination, I understood the existence of my dis-eases and the possibility of wellness. When I did, I became free to fulfill my purpose, inspired to reclaim my power and awaken to become at ease with life. Don't defer your wellness. Instead of saying I'm going to, say I will. The time is now. Attend to your wounds and your feelings in life. *Wellness Begins Inside.* Be well-heal.

AFTERWORD

Physical health is not a commodity to be bargained for. Nor can it be swallowed in the form of drugs and pills. It has to be earned through sweat.
—B. K. S. Iyengar

Are you alive? If so, be grateful. During the 2020 pandemic, I conceived *Wellness Begins Inside.* At that time, our lives were in imminent danger from a novel virus. SARS-CoV-2 and its variants Omicron, Delta, Delta AY.4.2, Beta, Alpha changed the world. It was a time when quarantine, ventilators, deaths, and disease became the norm. Mask wearing and social distancing changed us in unimaginable ways. It was also a time when we lost our jobs permanently, businesses closed forever, and worse, schools closed, causing irreparable damage to our children. Intense fear, anxiety, and even depression flourished. All of this chaos, including social unrest and violence, pushed the activation of our sympathetic nervous system, or stress response. We overate, over-zoomed, and binge on social media and television shows. For days on end, new and personal stories of Covid deaths held our minds hostage, with COVID-19 ranked as the third leading cause of death, disproportionately affecting minority communities. More than 900,000 people have died in the U.S. of Covid-19. Me, I lost the last three of my immediate family during Covid.

Even though they did not die from Covid, I believe they died from the effect of Covid.

Did you get Covid? Did you know someone who contracted Covid or even died from the virus? More than likely, you did? With all the ticker tape of deaths and ICU beds and ventilators' updates, Covid talk became anxiety-provoking. But even before Covid, this book has been in the making. The virus just became a signal of the importance of taking care of ourselves. Self-care stood out often during the contradictory medical advice and uncertainties in our day-to-day living through it all. Tele Med, Telehealth, and virtual living reveal the power of Covid but also our helplessness. Fear set in like rigor mortis.

One evening, I remember not feeling well and accessing the Tel-med system for the first time, only to doctor myself by taking my pulse and temperature while sensing this doctor's fear on the screen. I didn't have Covid. But it made me realize how absolutely essential it was for me to take charge of my health. When there is fear, there is no freedom.

Are we in the aftermath of this virus? Did we go back to sleep with the moderate cases and status, or are Covid deaths no longer reported? Can we come out of our caves? Do we ignore what has happened and go back to our usual way of living? Or commit to reducing some co-existing diseases by changing our way of life? If we're honest, even before the virus, many of us were suffering from chronic illnesses like high blood pressure, asthma, diabetes, and obesity, which worsen this disease. However, despite these comorbidities, we continue to gain weight and endure a heightened level of stress-related health problems, which compromise our immune system's capabilities, aggravate diseases, and threaten our wellness.

How do we reverse the harm not only from Covid but our

overall lifestyle choices? By practicing self-care. Learning to take care of ourselves translates into practice or a way of life that heals, not harms. In self-care, we practice self-love and mindfulness. We let go or unpack our emotional matters to allow energy to flourish. *Wellness Begins Inside* is an affirmation for self-care, which is not just about our food but thoughts, emotions, relationships, and lifestyle.

Of course, becoming healthy is a choice that takes willpower and courage. When you accept the challenge, life changes. As I've shared in this book, I come from a lineage of unhealthiness, but that didn't mean I had to inherit unhealthiness. I reclaimed my power from my upbringing, food story, and familiar diseases in my healing. As I did, my health and healing journey manifested-- I began to live to heal, live with purpose. I am Alive.

I AM ALIVE

I am alive. I am breathing. I am eating. I am moving. I am speaking. Actually, I feel good. My lungs rhythmically expand and contract, while my heart beats back and forth across my chest with a message—be alive. But do something with your aliveness.

I hear the message as I resist the urge to touch my face. Sometimes I forget. As I resist the urge to be around others that may destroy my aliveness. I sneeze and wonder. Still, I resist the urge to overthink, to become imbalance, to worry—to even question. Nowadays, as I hide in my bunker, I resist the urge to do so many things I used to do—because I am so damn happy that I am alive.

As I inhale through my left and right nostrils, I sense the fragility of life more than ever. And yet, a strange joy overwhelms me as I reflect on all that I have gone through in life. Life, as Hughes says, "ain't been no crystal stair." No stimulus, no support kept me alive. And while the past didn't kill me, this 27 to 34 kilobases coronavirus while in the ring goes for my nostrils against my 120 pounds. But I swerve to the right, then the left; I duck, I stumble, will Corona mess up my record in my aliveness? Place your bets.

Will it overtake my lungs, shorted my breath, and overheat my body? Hell no! Because I will fight back. Fight back with not only knowledge but also food. Fight back, knowing that I have a divine purpose and possess the spiritual powers to be alive. Within me, I hold the antidote, the antibodies to fight. As I sharpen my three weapons: Appreciate. Concentrate. Meditate. I am feeling doing, loving, speaking, seeing and understanding. As I fight energy with energy---I reclaim my crown, my halo, my power. I pray. I am alive. All thanks are due to the Creator, and my ancestors. Wellness Begins Inside. Àse

-Dr. Alston

REFERENCES

Abou El-Soud, Neveen Helmy (2009). Herbal Medicine in Ancient Egypt. *Journal of Medicinal Plants Research,* 4, no.2: 82–86. https://doi.org 10.5897/JMPR09.013

American College of Cardiology. (2020). "To Reap Heart Benefits of a Plant-Based Diet, Avoid Junk Food." March 18, 2020. https://www.acc.org/about-acc/press-releases/2020/03/18/09/26/to-reap-heart-benefits-of-a-plant-based-diet-avoid-junk-food.

Anpu, U.Shaka Nebu-Ra (2017). *Meditation for African Americans.* Igniting the Inner Light. Gye Name Publishing House.

Ashby, Muata (2002). "Kemetic Diet. Ancient African Wisdom for Health of Mind, Boddy and Spirit. Cruzian Mystic Books/ Sema Institute of Yoga.

Britannica, The Editors of Encyclopedia. "food". *Encyclopedia Britannica*, 24 Mar. 2020, https://www.britannica.com/topic/food. Accessed 15 February 2022.

Bloom, Martin. G. 2013. "92% of U.S. Population Have Vitamin Deficiency. Are You One of Them?" The Biostation. September 14). Retrieved May 2, 2022, from https://thebio-station.com/bioblog/do-you-have-vitamin-deficiency/

Bratskeir, Kate. (March 31, 2016). *How much water do I need*? HuffPost. Retrieved May 2, 2022, from https://www.huffpost.com/topic/how-much-water-do-i-need

Carlson, C. (April 23, 2020). *A runner's guide to sugar.* Women's Running. Retrieved May 2, 2022, from https://www.womensrunning.com/health/food/a-runners-guide-to-sugar/

Carroll, Abigail. (2013) "Three Squares, The Invention of the American Meal." Basic Books, pp.6.

Chinese Medicine. Johns Hopkins Medicine. Accessed May 2, 2022. https://www.hopkinsmedicine.org/health/wellness-and-prevention/chinese-medicine

Conason, A. (2012) *"Sugar Addiction." Psychology Today.* Posted October 12, 2012 *https://www.psychologytoday.com/us/blog/eating-mindfully/201204/sugar-addiction.* https://www.psychologytoday.com/us/blog/eating-mindfully/201204/sugar-addiction.

Daly, John. (2014). "What Is Etiquette and Where Did It Originate?" *Noozhawk.com Santa Barbara & Goleta Local News.* Published August 12, 2014. www.noozhawk.com/article/john_daly_etiquette_origins_20140812.

David, Rosalie. (2008). "The Art of Healing in Ancient Egypt: A Scientific Reappraisal." The Lancet. https://www.thelancet.com/journals/lancet/article/PIIS0140-6736(08)61749-3/fulltext. *The Lancet.*

De Bellefonds, C. (2020, November 6). *16 subtle symptoms you're eating too much sugar —.* Eat this not that. Retrieved May 4, 2022, from https://eatthisonline.org/too-much-sugar/

"Diabetes & Insulin Prescription/Medication Assistance." https://simplefill.com/diabetes-insulin-prescription-assistance/.

Expert Panel on Detection, Evaluation, and Treatment of High Blood Cholesterol in Adults. 2001. "Executive Summary of The Third Report of The National Cholesterol Education Program (NCEP) Expert Panel on Detection, Evaluation, and Treatment of High Blood Cholesterol in Adults (Adult Treatment Panel III)." *JAMA* 285 (19): 2486–2497. https://doi.org/10.1001/jama.285.19.2486.

Fernandez, Keith. (2019). "Regular as clockwork". Gulf News. September 16, 2019. https://gulfnews.com/uae/health/regular-as-clockwork-1.1568625949054

Frawley, D. (1999). Yoga & Ayurveda. *Self-Healing and Self-Realization. Lotus Press.*

Frey,Malia. (2017.). *7 SIGNS YOU'RE EATING TOO MUCH SALT.* Muscle and Fitnesshttps://www.muscleandfitness.com/nutrition/7-signs-you-re-eating-too-much-salt/.

Gerber, Richard. *Vibrational Medicine: The #1 Handbook of Subtle-Energy Therapies.* Bear & Co., 2001.

Glenn. Katie (2020, March 18). *To reap heart benefits of a plant-based diet, avoid junk food.* DoveMed. Retrieved May 3, 2022, from https://www.dovemed.com/current-medical-news/reap-heart-benefits-plant-based-diet-avoid-junk-food/

Griffin, Riley. (2020). "*Two Big Drug Flops Show How Health-Care Economics Have Changed.*" Last modified: January 10, 2020. https://www.bloombergquint.com/bq-blue-exclusive/these-big-drug-flops-show-how-healthcare-economics-have-changed

Guha, A. (2016). *What is the philosophy of Ayurvedic Medicine?* Taking Charge of Your Health & Wellbeing. Retrieved May 3, 2022, from https://www.takingcharge.csh.umn.edu/what-philosophy-ayurvedic-medicine

Hackensack Meridian Pascack Valley Medical Center. 2019. "Vitamins and Minerals to Strengthen Your Hair, Skin, and Nails." Hackensack Meridian Pascack Valley Medical Center (website). https://pascackmedicalcenter.com/news/vitamins-and-minerals-strengthen-your-hair-skin-and-nails.

"How Much Sugar Do You Eat? You May Be Surprised!" New Hampshire Department of Health and Human Services, Division of Public Health Services (website). https://www.dhhs.nh.gov/dphs/nhp/documents/sugar.pdf.

Hughes, L. 2019. "How Does Too Much Sugar Affect Your Body?" WebMD. https://www.webmd.com/diabetes/features/how-sugar-affects-your-body.

Infuse Wellness. 2020. "Mind, Body, Wellness: It's More than Exercising." Infuse Wellness. https://infusewellnessmichigan.com/mind-body-wellness-its-more-than-exercising/

Jenco, Melissa. 2016. "AHA: Limit Children's Sugar Consumption to 6 Teaspoons per Day." American Academy of Pediatrics (website). https://www.aappublications.org/news/2016/08/23/Sugar082316.

Lambert, Craig. 2004. "The Way We Eat Now." *Harvard Magazine*. https://harvardmagazine.com/2004/05/the-way-we-eat-now.html.

MacGregor, G. A., and H. E. de Wardener.1998. *Salt, Diet, and Health: Neptune's Poisoned Chalice: The Origins of High Blood Pressure*. Cambridge: Cambridge University Press.

Mayo Clinic Staff. 1998-2022. "A1C Test." Mayo Clinic (website). https://www.mayoclinic.org/tests-procedures/a1c-test/about/pac-20384643.

Nazish, N. (2021, December 10). *This is the best time to eat breakfast, according to a Dietitian*. Forbes. Retrieved May 3, 2022, from https://www.forbes.com/sites/nomanazish/2018/10/25/this-is-the-best-time-to-eat-breakfast-according-to-a-dietitian/

Nazish, Noma. (2018). "This Is The Best Time To Eat Breakfast, According To A Dietitian." Forbes.com. October 25, 2018. https://www.forbes.com/sites/nomanazish/2018/10/25/this-is-the-best-time-to-eat-breakfast-according-to-a-dietitian/

"Nutrients Research Paper." 2014. Study Mode Research. Published October 19, 2014. https://www.studymode.com/essays/Nutrients-61166524.html.

Olito, F. 2019. "What the Average Person Spends on Dining Out in Every State." Insider. Published August 12, 2019. https://www.businessinsider.com/what-people-spend-on-dining-out-2019-8.

Panagiotakos, D. (2021). "To Reap Heart Benefits of a Plant-Based Diet, Avoid Junk Food." ScienceCodex.com. Published May 4, 2021. https://www.sciencecodex.com/reap-heart-benefits-plant-based-diet-avoid-junk-food-643197.

Pankey, E. A. (2019). "Health Concerns Affecting African Americans." SummaHealth.com. November 15, 2019. https://www.summahealth.org/flourish/entries/2019/11/7-serious-health-concerns-affecting-african-americans.

Pincock, Stephen. (2011). "Boyd Swinburn: Combating Obesity at the Community Level." *The Lancet* 378, no. 9793: 804–14. (August 27, 2011.) https://doi.org/10.1016/S0140-6736(11)61364-0.

Preidt, R. 2020. "For Heart Health, Not All Plant-Based Diets Are Equal: Study." *U.S. News and World Report*. March 18, 2020. https://www.usnews.com/news/health-news/articles/2020-03-18/for-heart-health-not-all-plant-based-diets-are-equal-study.

Reynolds, L., A. Rodgers, and M. Sutherland. (2015). "Veganism in American Culture." n.d. Foodways in Focus. Accessed May 2, 2022. http://foodwaysinfocus.leadr.msu.edu/fall-2015/veganism-in-american-culture/

Roizen, M. F., M. Crupain, T. Spiker, and M. Shen. (2019). *What to Eat When: A Strategic Plan to Improve Your Health and Life through Food*. Washington, DC: National Geographic. Accessed May 2, 2022.

Sloan, A. E. (2018). "What, When, and Where America Eats." Institute of Food Technology. January 1, 2018. https://www.ift.org/news-and-publications/food-technology-magazine/issues/2018/january/features/americans-current-food-preferences.

Solan, M. (2019). "The Best Foods for Vitamins and Minerals." Harvard Health. August 17, 2021. https://www.health.harvard.edu/staying-healthy/the-best-foods-for-vitamins-and-minerals.

Staff Writer. (2020). "How Many Happy Meals Are Sold Each Day"? Reference. April 11, 2020. https://www.reference.com/world-view/many-happy-meals-sold-day-f433ed8686898e97.

Szalay, J. (2021, November 15). *What is protein?* LiveScience. Retrieved May 3, 2022, from https://www.livescience.com/53044-protein.html

Stass, Joanna. (2016). "What Happens to Your Body an Hour after Eating Sugar?" *Independent*. February 17, 2016. https://www.independent.co.uk/life-style/food-and-drink/features/what-happens-your-body-hour-after-eating-sugar-a6879026.html.

Stevens, E. "The Critical Reasons How We Eat Matters More Than WHAT." Whole Life Challenge. https://www.wholelifechallenge.com/the-critical-reasons-how-we-eat-matters-more-than-what/.

Stevens, E. (2022). "The Critical Reasons How We Eat Matters More Than WHAT." Whole Life Challenge. Accessed May 2, 2022. https://www.wholelifechallenge.com/the-critical-reasons-how-we-eat-matters-more-than-what/.

Stöppler, M. C. (2021). "Definition of Emotional Eating." Medicine Net. Reviewed on March 29, 2021. https://www.medicinenet.com/emotional_eating/definition.htm.

Sturm, R. (2005b) Childhood obesity – what we can learn from existing data on societal trends, part2, Preventing Chronic Disease, Retrieved April, 2007 from http://www.cdc.gov/pcd/issues/2005/apr/ 04_0039.htm.

Swinburn, B., Egger, G. and Raza, F. (1999) Dissecting obesogenic environments: The development and application of a framework for identifying and prioritizing environmental interventions for obesity, Preventive Medicine, 29, 6, 563–70.

Szalay, Jessie. McKelvie, Callum. (2021) "*What is Protein*?" LiveScience.com. November 15, 2021. https://www.livescience.com/53044_protein.html?_sm_au_=iVV7RtPJ2Q4WJq5b.

Tai, M. C. (2012). "An Oriental Understanding of Health." *Tzu Chi Medical Journal* 24 (2): 92–5. https://doi.org/10.1016/j.tcmj.2012.02.010.

Tamara. (2017). "6 Basic Nutrients Required for Your Child's Healthy Diet." The Pomegranate Mom. June 8, 2017. https://www.pomegranatemom.com/6-basic-nutrients-required-childs-healthy-diet/.

This Is the Best Time to Eat Breakfast, According To A Dietitian https://www.forbes.com/sites/nomanazish/2018/10/25/this-is-the-best-time-to-eat-breakfast-according-to-a-dietitian/

"To Reap Heart Benefits of a Plant-Based Diet, Avoid Junk Food." https://www.acc.org/about-acc/press-releases/2020/03/18/09/26/to-reap-heart-benefits-of-a-plant-based-diet-avoid-junk-food.

"Two Big Drug Flops Show How Health-Care Economics Have Changed." https://www.bloombergquint.com/bq-blue-exclusive/these-big-drug-flops-show-how-healthcare-economics-have-changed

U.S. Department of Health and Human Services. (n.d.). *Traditional chinese medicine: What you need to know.* National Center for Complementary and Integrative Health. Retrieved May 3, 2022, from https://www.nccih.nih.gov/health/traditional-chinese-medicine-what-you-need-to-kno

U.S. Department of Health and Human Services. (n.d.). *Vitamins and minerals for older adults.* National Institute on Aging. Retrieved May 3, 2022, from https://www.nia.nih.gov/health/vitamins-and-minerals-older-adults

Vitamins: Effective health care (EHC) program. Vitamins | Effective Health Care (EHC) Program. (n.d.). Retrieved

May 3, 2022, from https://effectivehealthcare.ahrq.gov/health-topics/vitamins

Wheeler, David. (2022). Nina Simone, I want A little sugar in my bowl. Occasional Glimpses of the Sublime. . Retrieved May 3, 2022, from https://www.occasional-glimpses.com/nina-simone-sings-i-want-a-little-sugar-in-my-bowl-1967/

White, P. (2015). 'The concept of diseases and health care in African traditional religion in Ghana', *HTS Teologiese Studies/Theological Studies* 71(3), Art. #2762, 7 pages. http://dx.doi.org/10.4102/ hts.v71i3.2762

Whitbread, D. (2020). "*Top 15 Foods Highest in Minerals.*" My Food Data. Accessed May 2, 2022.https://www.myfooddata.com/articles/high-mineral-foods.php

Why Eating on a Schedule May Improve Your Digestion? StopColonCancerNow.com. Published October 23, 2014. https://stopcoloncancernow.com/news/october-2014/why-eating-on-a-schedule-may-improve-your-digestion

Willey, J. (2022). "Pollution Linked to Heart Attacks and Strokes." DiscoverWalking.com. Accessed May 2, 2022. https://www.discoverwalking.com/blog/pollution-tied-to-heart-attacks-and-strokes.php

Willett, W., E. L. Giovannucci, and P. J. Skerrett. (2017). *Eat, Drink, and Be Healthy: The Harvard Medical School Guide to Healthy Eating.* New York: Free Press Paperbacks.

World Health Organization. (2022). What Is the WHO Definition of Health?. Accessed May 2, 2022.

World Health Organization. (2022). *Health and well-being.* World Health Organization. Retrieved May 3, 2022, from https://www.who.int/about/governance/constitution.

Why Eating on a Schedule May Improve Your Digestion? https://stopcoloncancernow.com/news/october-2014/why-eating-on-a-schedule-may-improve-your-digestion

Xue CC, Zhang AL, Greenwood KM, Lin V, Story DF. Traditional Chinese medicine: an update on clinical evidence. J Altern Complement Med. 2010 Mar;16(3):301-12. doi:10.1089/acm.2009.0293. PMID: 20192915

Zhang, Lin. (2019). "Short Overview of FDA Regulations and Guidance for the Traditional Chinese Medicine (TCM)" PharmaSources.com. October 15, 2019. https://www.pharmasources.com/news/57829.htm

Garden with green pepper

ABOUT THE AUTHOR

Dr. Alston is a psychologist, yogini, educator and author of "The Art of Feeling Good" and "Ase Yoga, Where Every Breath Counts."She also a cancer survivor, and writes from personal enlightenment. As an energy chef, she cooks every day not only for herself but others. With experiences spanning over two decades, she considers herself a warrior for health and healing.